The Harcourt Brace Casebook Series in Literature

"Master Harold" . . . and the boys

Athol Fugard

THE HARCOURT BRACE CASEBOOK SERIES IN LITERATURE
Series Editors: Laurie G. Kirszner and Stephen R. Mandell

DRAMA
Athol Fugard
"Master Harold" . . . *and the boys*

William Shakespeare
Hamlet

POETRY
Emily Dickinson
A Collection of Poems

Langston Hughes
A Collection of Poems

SHORT STORIES
Charlotte Perkins Gilman
"The Yellow Wallpaper"

John Updike
"A & P"

Eudora Welty
"A Worn Path"

The Harcourt Brace Casebook Series in Literature
Series Editors: Laurie G. Kirszner and Stephen R. Mandell

"Master Harold" . . .
and the boys

Athol Fugard

Contributing Editor

Kim J. Allison
Texas Woman's University

THOMSON
™
HEINLE

Australia Canada Mexico Singapore Spain United Kingdom United States

THOMSON

✳ ™

HEINLE

The Harcourt Brace Series in Literature
"Master Harold"... and the Boys
Athol Fugard

Publisher: *Christopher P. Klein*
Executive Editor: *Michael Rosenberg*
Developmental Editor: *Katie Frushour*
Project Editor: *Kylie E. Johnston*
Production Manager: *Melinda Esco*
Art Director: *Vicki Whistler*

For more information contact Heinle, 25 Thomson Place, Boston, MA 02210 USA,
or you can visit our Internet site at http://www.heinle.com

For permission to use material from this text or product contact us:
Tel   1-800-730-2214
Fax   1-800-730-2215
Web   www.thomsonrights.com

ISBN: 0-1550-5483-X

Library of Congress Catalog Card Number: 97-70035

ABOUT THE SERIES

The Harcourt Brace Casebook Series in Literature has its origins in our anthology *Literature: Reading, Reacting, Writing* (Third Edition, 1997), which in turn arose out of our many years of teaching college writing and literature courses. The primary purpose of each Casebook in the series is to offer students a convenient, self-contained reference tool that they can use to complete a research project for an introductory literature course.

In choosing subjects for the Casebooks, we draw on our own experience in the classroom, selecting works of poetry, fiction, and drama that students like to read, discuss, and write about and that teachers like to teach. Unlike other collections of literary criticism aimed at student audiences, The Harcourt Brace Casebook Series in Literature features short stories, groups of poems, or plays (rather than longer works, such as novels) because these are the genres most often taught in college-level Introduction to Literature courses. In selecting particular authors and titles, we focus on those most popular with students and those most accessible to them.

To facilitate student research—and to facilitate instructor supervision of that research—each Casebook contains all the resources students need to produce a documented research paper on a particular work of literature. Every Casebook in the series includes the following elements:

- A comprehensive **introduction** to the work, providing social, historical, and political background. This introduction helps students to understand the work and the author in the context of a particular time and place. In particular, the introduction enables students to appreciate customs, situations, and events that may have contributed to the author's choice of subject matter, emphasis, or style.

- A **headnote**, including birth and death dates of the author; details of the work's first publication and its subsequent publication history, if relevant; details about the author's life; a summary of the author's career; and a list of key published works, with dates of publication.

- The most widely accepted version of the **literary work,** along with the explanatory footnotes students will need to understand unfamiliar terms and concepts or references to people, places, or events.

- **Discussion questions** focusing on themes developed in the work. These questions, designed to stimulate critical thinking and discussion, can also serve as springboards for research projects.

- Several extended **research assignments** related to the literary work. Students may use these assignments exactly as they appear in the Casebook, or students or instructors may modify the assignments to suit their own needs or research interests.

- A diverse collection of traditional and non-traditional **secondary sources,** which may include scholarly articles, reviews, interviews, memoirs, newspaper articles, historical documents, and so on. This resource offers students access to sources they might not turn to on their own—for example, a popular song that inspired a short story, a story that was the original version of a play, a legal document that sheds light on a work's theme, or two different biographies of an author—thus encouraging students to look beyond the obvious or the familiar as they search for ideas. Students may use only these sources, or they may supplement them with sources listed in the Casebook's bibliography (see below).

- An annotated model **student research paper** drawing on several of the Casebook's secondary sources. This paper uses MLA parenthetical documentation and includes a Works Cited list conforming to MLA style.

- A comprehensive **bibliography** of print and electronic sources related to the work. This bibliography offers students an opportunity to move beyond the sources in the Casebook to other sources related to a particular research topic.

- A concise **guide to MLA documentation,** including information on what kinds of information require documentation (and what kinds do not); a full explanation of how to construct parenthetical references and how to place them in a paper; sample parenthetical reference formats for various kinds of sources used in papers about literature; a complete explanation of how to assemble a List of Works Cited, accompanied by sample works cited entries (including formats for documenting electronic sources); and guidelines for using explanatory notes (with examples).

By collecting all this essential information in one convenient place, each volume in The Harcourt Brace Casebook Series in Literature responds to the needs of both students and teachers. For students, the Casebooks offer convenience, referentiality, and portability that make the process of doing research easier. Thus, the Casebooks recognize what students already know: that Introduction to Literature is not their only class and that the literature research paper is not their only assignment. For instructors, the Casebooks offer a rare combination of flexibility and control in the classroom. For example, teachers may choose to assign one Casebook or more than one; thus, they have the option of having all students in a class write about the same work or having different groups of students, or individual students, write about different works. In addition, instructors may ask students to use only the secondary sources collected in the Casebook, thereby controlling students' use of (and acknowledgement of) sources more closely, or they may encourage students to seek both print and electronic sources beyond those included in the Casebook. By building convenience, structure, and flexibility into each volume, we have designed The Harcourt Brace Casebook Series in Literature to suit a wide variety of teaching styles and research interests. The Casebooks have made the research paper an easier project for us and a less stressful one for our students; we hope they will do the same for you.

Laurie G. Kirszner
Stephen R. Mandell
Series Editors

"Master Harold" . . . *and the boys* was written by Athol Fugard during the darkest days of apartheid in South Africa. At the time he wrote this play, he could not have known that in a little more than a decade, the political system that strictly segregated the population of South Africa on the basis of race would no longer exist. Even more amazing, this entrenched racist society would change without a shot being fired, and the president of the new system would be a person who himself had been imprisoned for revolutionary activities.

When reading *"Master Harold"* . . . *and the boys,* one question that comes to mind is whether the play—which was written as a condemnation of the racist policies of South Africa—remains relevant now that apartheid has been abolished. Although answering this question is not easy, one thing is certain: *"Master Harold"* . . . *and the boys* retains its power to move audiences deeply. The main characters—Sam, Hally, and Willie—are involved in a deeply satisfying yet troubled relationship that forces each to examine what it means to be human and what it means to live in a society where privilege is doled out on the basis of race. In growing up, Hally has to face issues that will determine his relationship not only to Sam and Willie, but also to his parents and to his community. The choice he faces is one that most of us face at one time or another—whether to accept the world as we find it or to reject intolerance and bigotry and try to make the world a better place.

The sources included in the Casebook do not speak with a single voice. Some praise *"Master Harold"* . . . *and the boys* while others debate the play's merits or even challenge Fugard's ideas about class and race. All, however, present ideas that will stimulate your thinking and in the end help you develop original ideas about the play. After all, the purpose of these sources is not to lead you by the hand, but to offer you a possible reading of a work and challenge you to react. In order to help you develop your own ideas about *"Master Harold"* . . . *and the boys,* we have selected eight sources that shed light on its characters and themes. Some of these sources are autobiographical, while others have a historical, psychological, racial, or political focus:

- Durbach, Errol. " *'Master Harold'* . . . *and the boys:* Athol Fugard and the Psychopathology of Apartheid." Durbach offers a psychological reading of the play, concentrating on the effect that apartheid has on Hally, Sam, and Willie, and presents a unique perspective on the complex psychological relationship that exists among the three characters.

- Vandenbroucke, Russell. "Fathers and Son: *'Master Harold'* . . . *and the boys.*" This essay focuses on the father-son relationship between Sam and Hally. Going beyond the scope of Durbach's essay, Vandenbroucke explores the autobiographical elements of the play—especially the relationship of Fugard to his own father and to a gardener who worked for the family.

- Solomon, Alisa. "'Look at History': An Interview with Zakes Mokae." Zakes Mokae, the South African actor who played the role of Sam in the original Yale Repertory production of *"Master Harold"* . . . *and the boys,* offers a unique insight into the play as well as into the condition of blacks in South Africa at the time the play was written. In addition, Mokae provides historical and cultural background relating to the role of apartheid in South African history.

- von Staden, Heinrich. "An Interview with Athol Fugard." Fugard discusses his life in South Africa as well as the specific South African context for the play.

- Fugard, Athol. From *Notebooks 1960–1977.* These notes clarify some of the autobiographical information Fugard mentions in his interviews with von Staden—specifically, the nature of the relationship between Fugard and Sam, a gardener who worked for Fugard's family. (Vandenbroucke also mentions this relationship.)

- Mshengu. "Political Theater in South Africa and the Work of Athol Fugard." This article is a foil for the articles in the Casebook that praise Fugard. Here Mshengu makes the point that, contrary to popular opinion, Fugard was not the only playwright in South Africa fighting against apartheid. Moreover, contends Mshengu, Fugard's race (white) and class (privileged) caused him to ignore the people's struggle going on around him.

- Post, Robert M. "Racism in Athol Fugard's *'Master Harold'* . . . *and the boys*." Unlike Mshengu, Post sees Fugard as confronting the racism that was everywhere in South Africa. While acknowledging the autobiographical elements of the play, Post contends that the play's universal message is that racism is intolerable, wherever and in whatever form it exists.

- Jordan, John O. "Life in the Theatre: Autobiography, Politics, and Romance in *'Master Harold'* . . . *and the boys*." This article asserts that the emphasis on the autobiographical and confessional aspects of the play have distorted its political and theatrical significance. According to Jordan, the split between Hally and Sam actually represents Fugard's willingness to accept the coming of age of the black theater in South Africa.

In addition to the articles above, we have also included a student paper in the Casebook. We chose this paper not only because it illustrates MLA documentation style and format, but also because it shows how the various sources in the book can be used to write about *"Master Harold"* . . . *and the boys*. The student writer, Joshua Miron, examines one of the major points of debate in the play—why Sam fails to react after Hally spits in his face. Joshua begins his paper by giving several possible explanations for Sam's inaction and then goes on to offer his own interpretation of the event. Notice that throughout the paper the ideas of the critics supplement and support Joshua's own ideas. It is Joshua's voice and his voice alone that dominates the discussion.

ACKNOWLEDGMENTS

No project as ambitious as the Casebook series happens without the help of many talented and dedicated people. First, we would like to thank everyone who was involved with the first and subsequent editions of *Literature: Reading, Reacting, Writing*. It was while working on this book that we developed and refined the casebook idea. Next, we would like to thank the people who worked with us on the *"Master Harold"* . . . *and the boys* Casebook: the developmental editor, Katie Frushour; the production manager, Melinda Esco; the art director, Vicki Whistler; and the project editor, Kylie Johnston. Finally, we would like to thank Michael Rosenberg, who suggested the idea of a Casebook series, and without whose enthusiastic help and support this series would never have come into being.

CONTENTS

Sample Student Research Paper

An annotated essay in which student Joshua Miron explores the factors influencing Sam's response to Hally's affront.

Bibliography

A bibliography of print and electronic sources, including a list of Fugard's plays and other works, biographical profiles of and interviews with the author, criticism and commentary on Fugard's works, and resources for understanding South Africa's rich history.

Appendix: Documenting Sources 159

Introduction

South Africa: The Rise and Fall of Apartheid

Over the past three hundred years, South Africa has experienced tumultuous changes in its ethnic diversity, its race relations, its economic stability, and its political ideology. In order to understand *"Master Harold"... and the boys,* it is necessary to know something about this history—in particular, about apartheid, the repressive government policy of racial segregation.

Originally a territory inhabited by the Khoi-khoi (Hottentots) and San (Bushmen), South Africa changed significantly as white settlers appropriated it. Dutch colonists, who brought with them the concept of white domination, were among the first to settle in the southern territory, establishing Cape Town in 1652. Establishing rule over the Cape of Good Hope, the Dutch settlers defined the relationship between whites and natives as that of master and servant. Native Africans were forced into slavery alongside slaves imported from Indonesia, India, Madagascar, and Mozambique.

White dominance in South Africa gained strength as Britain seized control of the Cape colony in 1795. British colonists waged an aggressive campaign to displace black Africans from South African lands, a campaign that became increasingly brutal as gold was discovered on tribal lands. Britain also encouraged and funded a mass immigration of primarily lower-middle-class European citizens from England, Wales, Ireland, and Scotland. This influx of immigrants continued throughout the nineteenth century, increasing the white presence in southern Africa and, in turn, provoking savage wars. Meanwhile, the once ruling Dutch settlers, who had renamed themselves Afrikaners, struggled to regain power. Hostility between the British and the Dutch settlers culminated in the Boer War (1899–1902), which resulted in Britain maintaining its domination of South Africa.

By the start of the twentieth century, two hundred years of white domination had set the precedent for the decades to follow. Although the British had abolished slavery in 1830, they had introduced into South

Africa an equally devastating capitalistic economic system in which whites reaped the riches of black labor. As British reign spread throughout the southern territories of Africa, the white minority, dispersed among four colonies, unified under a constitution aimed at disfranchising Africans and those of mixed race. Taking command in 1910, the new white-controlled Union of South Africa began the task of institutionalizing its policies of racial discrimination and segregation.

In 1913, the Union approved the Natives Land Act and ordered military troops to forcibly remove hundreds of thousands of Africans from the countryside. Mine workers, too, were segregated—the Africans relegated to prison-like quarters—and the 1923 Natives (Urban Areas) Act extended the policies of segregation to urban areas so that whites and Africans would be restricted to separate living and working places. All confiscated lands were then redistributed among whites. By the 1930s, several political parties had emerged in South Africa, with the all-white National Party becoming the most formidable. In response to the National Party's increasing strength, African intellectuals organized as well, forming the African National Congress (ANC), which vowed to fight for the African majority's political, personal, and economic rights and freedoms.

By the 1940s, South Africa's economy was booming. Industrialization had expanded substantially during the Second World War, and black South Africans, especially, were benefiting from increased job opportunities in urban areas, from rising wages, and from trade union gains. However, as masses of disfranchised South Africans moved to urban areas to secure industrial jobs, rural areas became increasingly impoverished. Afrikaner farmers, descendants of early Dutch settlers, began to suffer the economic consequences of this migration: the lack of cheap black labor meant lower earnings for Afrikaner farmers. Consequently, Afrikaners, second only to English-speaking whites in the racial hierarchy, began to demand tighter control over black Africans. Fearing that black protests in urban areas would convince English-speaking whites to further jeopardize Afrikaner agriculture and businesses by granting subsequent reforms for black South Africans, Afrikaners began to unify and demand more political power in order to strengthen their economic status.

Afrikaners unified their interests in the Afrikaner Nationalist Alliance and began discussing effective strategies for addressing the "native question" and the increasing number of Afrikaner poor. Professionals, clergy, intellectuals, and civil servants were united in new advocacy of the ideological principle of apartheid (Afrikaans for "apartness"). Apartheid had as its foundation the assumption that Africa was made up of four racial groups—the whites, including the English-speaking and Afrikaners; the Africans, black descendants of indigenous peoples; the Indians, people from Asia and India; and the Coloreds, persons of mixed race. According to apartheid ideology, the white race was the only civilized race and was therefore entitled to better services and facilities and, more significantly, to control of the state.

As a means of initiating apartheid goals, Afrikaner leaders advocated complete segregation of the races, not only to preserve Afrikaner culture and identity but also to upgrade Afrikaner political and economic power to equal that of English-speaking whites. Apartheid appealed to both workers' organizations and to such powerful, extremist Afrikaner organizations as the Afrikaner Broederbond, the South African Bureau of Racial Affairs (SABRA), and the Dutch Reformed Church (DRC). Aligning themselves with the National Party, Afrikaner leaders set out to take control of parliament and institute their strategy.

After its victory in the 1948 elections, the National Party created a complex bureaucracy that employed mass legislation and extreme military force to tighten their control over nonwhite South Africans, to enforce absolute racial segregation, to eliminate urbanization by nonwhites, and to establish state control of the economic and educational systems.

In 1950, the National Party government in Pretoria began the most profound stage of institutionalizing apartheid, enacting an unprecedented number of laws for strictly enforcing segregation of the races. To ensure effective separation of the races, the government of Pretoria ratified the Population Registration Act (1950), which mandated the classification of each individual's ethnicity. In the same year, the government passed the Group Areas Act, which designated specific zones within urban areas in which South African blacks, Coloreds, and Indians could live and work. As South Africans' ethnic identities were determined, nonwhite urban residents were removed to shantytowns where basic services and facilities were absent. Simultaneously, the government began mass removals of South African blacks to "homelands," eradicating all-black communities throughout the countryside. Conditions in the homelands deteriorated as they became dangerously overpopulated, and poverty and disease reached epidemic proportions.

Increasingly, African blacks attempted to escape the impoverished homelands, and many men left their families behind to search for work in the industrialized cities. Fearing that nonwhites in urban areas would displace white South Africans, the National Party swiftly intensified "pass laws." Originally introduced in the eighteenth century, pass laws required African blacks to obtain a pass, or official document, in order to travel from their homelands to urban areas. By 1930, any African who entered a town had twenty-four hours to attain a pass from the town's official, and any African without a pass would be forced to leave the town or would be jailed. Black men were also obliged to carry work passes signed by their employers to prove the legitimacy of their presence outside of black shantytowns. Any Black African caught in a white area without such a pass would be denied further employment in white urban areas and could be arrested or expelled from the city. Each year, over a hundred thousand Africans were arrested for violations of pass laws; between 1975 and 1976, the number of arrests reached a high of 381,858.

In another move to isolate and stigmatize nonwhite Africans, the government made fraternization across racial lines illegal. Outlawing intermarriage and sexual contact between races, two phenomena that would have undermined the residential segregation laws, the National Party enacted the Prohibition of Mixed Marriages Act (1949) and the Immorality Act (1950). These two legislative acts, along with the military's strict enforcement of the Population Registration Act and Group Areas Act, devastated Black communities as families were torn apart.

Having established the white race as superior under apartheid, the National Party set into motion a policy of segregating all public facilities. Beginning in 1948, signs indicating "White Only" areas and services were posted throughout South Africa. Among the many segregated facilities were public transportation and parks, elevators, restaurants and cafes, hotels, cinemas and theaters, schools and universities, and government offices. This division of public facilities was made into an official state law in 1953, when the parliament passed the Reservation of Separate Amenities Act.

Once segregation was firmly in place, the National Party turned its attention to the suppression of antiapartheid sentiments and to the teaching of the virtues of white dominance. One of the first laws enacted to suppress apartheid opposition, the Suppression of Communism Act of 1950, prohibited any acts or strategies that did, or could possibly, promote political, social, or economic changes. Any behavior or mode of thought that encouraged disorder or unlawful acts was also forbidden. This ambiguous law allowed the minister of justice to ban any person posing a threat to the state's control. Banned persons were placed under virtual house arrest and could not appeal the minister's decision or communicate with any individuals or organizations in any way.

The Suppression of Communism Act also reinforced the Entertainments Act of 1931, which gave the government authority to censor films and public entertainment. Along with segregating theater and cinema audiences, the government strictly controlled subject matter and scenes, eliminating in particular any scenes that portrayed intermingling of races. Likewise, this legislation empowered the government to censor, or ban, any publication that challenged national order. Authors who commented on or illustrated the negative effects of South Africa's racial discrimination faced potential bannings and imprisonment. Those authors who were not imprisoned or exiled had their passports revoked and were placed under house arrest. Thus, by the mid-1960s, the Suppression of Communism Act had resulted in innumerable bannings of publications, arrests and convictions of journalists, and forced closures of newspapers.

In 1953, the parliament ratified the equally onerous Public Safety Act, which authorized the government' s use of brute force—already common in South Africa—to coerce nonwhites' adherence to the many legislative acts passed under apartheid. This act gave the government the power to arrest any individuals or members of organizations it considered a threat. Moreover, the government could declare a state of emergency anytime, anywhere, and could thus deploy armed troops to quell resistance.

At this time, the government also set into motion its mission of formally instilling the apartheid sensibility into South African society. First on the government's agenda of control was the educational system and the instruction of African blacks, which had previously been left to Christian missionaries. The government acquired control over education in 1953 through the ratification of the Bantu Education Act, which allowed the government to reinforce the concept of white privilege among white and Afrikaner primary-school students. To initiate its plans, the government established separate public school systems for whites, Afrikaners, and nonwhite Africans and proceeded to inculcate students with apartheid ideology through racially biased, government-approved textbooks and curriculum. By indoctrinating the African, Colored, and Indian students with the doctrines of white dominance, the National Party proposed to produce a new generation of South Africans who would envision life under apartheid as normal. In this way, the government hoped to thwart future resistance to state control.

With the state's administration of primary schools advancing according to plan, the government extended its control over the educational system to South African universities. When the parliament passed the 1959 Extension of University Education Act, the government closed a number of well-established universities; founded separate colleges for Africans, Coloreds, Indians, and Zulu students; and ordered that black students could only be admitted into universities with the permission of a cabinet minister.

To counter any remaining antiestablishment ideals, the government began a propaganda campaign aimed at domestic and foreign audiences. Several of South Africa's white nationalist prime ministers falsified reports of South African domestic affairs in speeches at home and abroad. Illustrated brochures promoting the national perspective were distributed overseas, and the African Department of Information bribed foreign journalists to write articles that would boost South Africa's reputation. The South African government also funded *The Citizen*, which advocated progovernment values to South African readers; at the same time, antiapartheid newspapers were banned and their journalists arrested. Eventually, with South Africans forbidden to listen to foreign radio, read foreign publications, or watch foreign films, the government established its own broadcasting system. The South African Broadcasting Corporation (SABC), which broadcast Afrikaans and English programming only, had as its main order of business the dissemination of official nationalist propaganda.

The magnitude of the government censorship, apartheid propaganda, and segregation took its toll on South African society. Whites soon perceived apartheid society to be the norm. Restricted to their own areas, most whites never saw how the Coloreds, Asians, Indians, and blacks lived, and only a select few spoke any African language. Moreover, government policy systematically favored Afrikaners; many were recruited into its enormous bureaucracy as public employees, and many held executive offices. Afrikaner poor received government support through a welfare system created specifically for them, and Afrikaner businesses were awarded the most important government contracts. Given superior social services and economic support, the majority of whites were, not surprisingly, unaware of the racial inequality plaguing their country.

In contrast, disfranchised Africans recognized the government's racial discrimination but started organizing in opposition to the National Party's policies. During the 1950s and 1960s, antiapartheid organizations emerged in force, operating at various levels of South African society. Foremost among such political organizations was the African National Congress (ANC), which began reacting to the multitude of legislative acts that discriminated against South African blacks.

Openly opposing white dominance, the ANC, in collaboration with the South African Indian Congress, launched a nonviolent passive-resistance campaign, the Defiance Campaign of Unjust Laws, in 1952. Increasingly, however, African blacks taking part in defiant demonstrations were arrested and sentenced to prison for their overt opposition to the government. Recognizing the extreme punishment threatening the activists—made clear by the 1953 Criminal Laws Amendment, which designated flogging and extensive imprisonment as the punishment for defying laws—the ANC called off the campaign. Two years later, the ANC created the Congress of the People, whose Freedom Charter proposed granting Africans legal and labor equality; freedom of speech, religion, movement, and assembly; and the right to vote.

In 1956, one year after the adoption of the Freedom Charter, the government charged more than one hundred ANC members with high treason and communistic conspiracy. At the same time, internal divisions began to increase within the organization as ANC members began to debate the effectiveness of civil disobedience and the potential power to be gained by including white activists in their struggle. By 1956, the ANC's affiliate, the Youth League, had formed its own militant organization, the Africanist. And as the trials of arrested ANC members continued throughout the next five years, Robert Sobukwe, a Bantu instructor, withdrew from the ANC to form the Pan Africanist Congress (PAC), a multiracial organization.

In 1960, the PAC launched widespread demonstrations against pass laws, instigating work stoppages and leading large assemblies of nonwhite South Africans outside police stations. During one such demonstration in Sharpesville, near Johannesburg, police surrounded protesters and opened fire on the crowd, killing sixty-seven Africans and wounding nearly two hundred others. During this same year, the government used army reserves to ban the ANC and PAC and to arrest more than eighteen thousand demonstrators, along with ANC and PAC leaders. Four years later, Nelson Mandela, along with other ANC and PAC leaders, was sentenced to life in prison.

Meanwhile, as universities experienced an influx of Black African students, student organizations were leading their own demonstrations against apartheid. Shortly after the enactment of the University Extension Act, the white-run National Union of South African Students (NUSAS) began demonstrating at universities, including the white, English-language universities of Cape Town and Witwatersrand. NUSAS protesters challenged, among other things, the racial segregation of university students and the government's exclusion of blacks from well-established universities.

NUSAS opposition was soon augmented by the protests of its breakaway organization, the South African Student Organization (SASO). SASO, established in 1968 by Steve Biko and other African blacks, professed a strict policy of noninvolvement of whites in order to generate unity among all black Africans who had suffered under white domination. Even though SASO called for the reform of the current system of racial discrimination, its most significant contribution to the antiapartheid opposition movement was the development of "Black Consciousness." As defined by Steve Biko, Black Consciousness is "in essence the realization by the black man of the need to rally together with his brothers around the cause of their oppression—the blackness of their skin—and to operate as a group in order to rid themselves of the shackles that bind them to perpetual servitude." Functioning on this principle, Black Consciousness emerged as an intellectual movement that encouraged African blacks to emancipate themselves from the mental acceptance of white domination and form a positive ethnic identity. By the 1970s, the Black Consciousness movement extended beyond the universities, pervading public schools and generating widespread student objections to the policies of apartheid.

In 1976, for example, protesting against the many required classes taught in Afrikaans, public-school students demonstrated in Soweto. The police descended on the protesting students and killed a thirteen-year-old African student, an act that generated nationwide student demonstrations against the government. Police reacted to the ensuing demonstrations with extreme violence that resulted in the deaths of over five hundred people—134 of them under age eighteen. Additional government retaliation included the banning of NUSAS in 1973 and of SASO in 1977, and the arrest, beating, and eventual murder of SASO's founder, Steve Biko. In response to the violent tactics of South African police, students (women as well as men) joined guerrilla training camps outside South Africa.

By the 1970s, many people, both black and white, realized that the policies of apartheid were destroying South African society. Protest culture had permeated all levels of South African society as men, women, and children staged large-scale uprisings in hopes of liberating South Africa from race and class discrimination. From intellectuals to the uneducated, from professionals to the unemployed, from the elite to the poverty stricken, South Africans voiced their dissatisfaction with apartheid ideology, legislation, and military force. Even some Afrikaner business leaders, along with the clergy and intellectuals who had once supported apartheid, denounced the system as immoral and ineffective.

Afrikaner antiapartheid sentiments continued to grow throughout the 1980s, and thousands of black and white South Africans staged open demonstrations against race and class discrimination. Nonwhite Africans boycotted schools, workplaces, and public transportation. And by 1983, six hundred South African organizations had joined forces to create the United Democratic Front (UDF). A coalition of trade unions, community groups, and organizations for students, youths, and women, the UDF endorsed the

Freedom Charter and planned to eliminate homelands. The UDF used its mixed-race collective to actively oppose apartheid. Advocating the replacement of the national ideology with a democracy, the UDF soon emerged as the most popular internal opposition movement in South Africa. The tremendous mobilization of the UDF, along with widespread work stayaways and black African protests opposing rent hikes, gave rise to an extensive police crackdown. In 1984, police arrested and detained UDF members and officials, thousands of black and white protesters, community employees, and church members under the authority of the Internal Securities Act of 1982.

The Internal Securities Act authorized police to detain an unindicted individual indefinitely, as a preventive measure or for interrogation. The government had instituted the Internal Securities Act to eliminate the intensifying opposition to the government and to quell South Africa's escalating violence. However, police behavior nullified any possibility of reducing resistance or violence, for police interrogators tortured and killed detainees at will. Consequently, violence in South African townships continued to escalate. Citizens aggressively resisted police and soldiers, while African children, having been socialized into vandalism and violence, established bloodthirsty rival gangs. As these youth gangs assassinated black collaborators and informants by igniting gasoline-drenched tires placed around their victims' necks, vigilante groups went on indiscriminate killing sprees, spraying bullets from the windows of cars.

In 1986, with police finding lawlessness unmanageable, South Africa's prime minister, Pieter Willem Botha, proclaimed a state of emergency and deployed more than five thousand soldiers to aid police in South African townships. Bannings, arrests, and detentions multiplied, and tens of thousands of victims were tortured and assassinated by security police and interrogators. Black South Africans had no refuge from the new powers of soldiers and police; even in their homes, citizens were attacked with tear gas and whips. Police also possessed the authority to impose curfews, to restrict funeral ceremonies, and to enforce the censorship of any subversive statements.

During this state of emergency, the Directorate of Publications devised a broad definition of censurable material. Police were advised to seize any material that might be considered offensive by any South African or that might endanger the order of the state. Accordingly, police began banning and seizing books, newspapers, and pamphlets from publishers, booksellers, and authors. Those persons accused of creating or selling "subversive" materials faced fines or jail terms, if not both. As their only recourse, novelists and playwrights, including Alan Paton, Andre Brink, and Nadine

Gordimer as well as Athol Fugard, were forced to publish their works overseas to evade police retaliation.

South Africa's state of emergency did not go unnoticed abroad. International newscasts televised scenes of extreme police brutality and unwarranted military assaults on black South Africans. The media's coverage of South Africa's race war instigated countless foreign protests against apartheid that eventually caused foreign countries, including the United States and several European countries, to begin pressuring the South African government to end apartheid. Increasingly, foreign governments imposed trade sanctions against South Africa. Western business leaders within South Africa and foreign financiers of South African banking and trade began to call for government concessions to nonwhite African demands. At the same time, as the South African economy began to decline, hundreds of Western investors and businesses withdrew their financial support from South Africa. By the close of the 1980s, diminishing foreign investments and trade sanctions augmented by internal work boycotts drove the South African economy into a depression.

As the country approached the 1989 elections, years of domestic unrest and loss of economic viability had diminished the government's power and seriously undermined the National Party's power. Because the majority of antiapartheid officials had been banned, exiled, or imprisoned, leaders of the clergy—including Desmond Tutu, whose activism won him the Nobel Peace Prize in 1984—had taken over the leadership of the antiapartheid movement. Under the clergy's direction, the apartheid opposition movement had reached revolutionary proportions. In this climate, Desmond Tutu and other antiapartheid clergy called for Christians to boycott the 1989 elections.

When the election votes were tallied, the National Party had, surprisingly, once again won the majority of legislative seats, with Frederik Willem de Klerk succeeding Botha as the party leader and prime minister. However, the National Party's faith in the system of apartheid had diminished. When de Klerk took command of the party, he began to repeal apartheid legislation. Among the first laws to be renounced were the Land Acts, the Group Area Acts, and the Separate Amenities Act. In 1990, Nelson Mandela and three thousand other political prisoners were released from prison, and by the end of 1991, several political organizations, including ANC and PAC, were no longer banned. Apartheid's potency had diminished, and education and labor gained some freedom from white dominance.

As de Klerk began the process of reform, South Africans appeared to be on the road to freedom and democracy. In April of 1991, the ANC, led by Nelson Mandela, published a tract of constitutional precepts designed to aid in the creation of an interim government and, eventually, of a democratic South Africa. The ANC and the South African government subsequently began negotiations to establish new policies for political and social reform. But even as the two political powers managed peaceful interactions, South Africa was increasingly suffering the consequences of new uncertainty about its political future.

These tremendous political and social changes evoked fear throughout the South African population, intensifying the volatile nature of the country's race relations. Violence, both political and criminal, soon exceeded that of the 1980s. Between 1991 and 1993, more than ten thousand South Africans were killed during political violence, but these numbers paled in comparison to the increase in serious criminal acts. Fires, explosions, stonings, murders, rapes, and beatings permeated everyday life as South African blacks fought among themselves and white revolutionaries retaliated against the new reforms for blacks.

Considering de Klerk a traitor to his race, many white South Africans devised strategies to thwart the progress of negotiations and deracialization. Right-wing Afrikaners, believing themselves displaced by the end of apartheid, rebelled against the prospect of racial equality. Neo-Nazi groups such as the Afrikaner Resistance Movement (AWB), formed in 1973, began to emerge as powerful adversaries, instigating clashes between blacks and destroying the property of the newly liberated ethnic groups. Afrikaner activists began to demand an Afrikaner homeland free from potential black rule. Meanwhile, the passionate struggle between the supporters of the ANC and the Inkatha Freedom Party (IFP), a Zulu ethnic movement, spread from Natal to South Africa, evoking murderous clashes among supporters and resulting in massacres of innocent black workers on commuter trains.

Finally, in September of 1991, after months of on-and-off talks, the ANC, IFP, and South African government signed the National Peace Accord. Although the disorder continued, the signing of this agreement allowed negotiations to proceed. At the Conference for a Democratic South Africa (CODESA) in December, both the National Party and the ANC proposed their versions of the constitution; however, no agreement could be reached. Despite continuing disagreement between negotiators, the CODESA did establish the right of South Africans to participate in a nonracial election.

Debates about the issue of open elections continued for approximately two years, but finally the political powers agreed on the date for the first postapartheid election. Between April 26 and 28 of 1994, South Africans of every ethnic background participated in the nation's first multiethnic election. During these three days, more than seventeen million citizens cast their votes, the majority of them for the first time in their lives. On the second day of the election, the ANC and the National Party introduced their plan for a new constitution and a new flag while South African voters lined up at the more than nine thousand polling stations. Virtually free of violence, the election was viewed as a success.

Within one week of the election, the ANC, having won 62.6 percent of the votes and the majority of the legislative seats, celebrated its victory. The ANC electoral victory ushered in South Africa's coalition government—made up of ANC, National Party, and IFP delegates—with Nelson Mandela as the interim president. On May 6, 1994, Mandela named Thabo Mbeki and F. W. de Klerk as deputy presidents and announced seventeen members of his cabinet. Four days later, Mandela was inaugurated into the office of president, observed by a massive crowd, which included United States political leaders and such notable African-Americans as Maya Angelou and Coretta Scott King.

Shortly after the inaugural ceremonies, the new interim parliament undertook the task of reforming apartheid's legacy. Within the first year of operation, the coalition government adopted the Reconstruction and Development Plan (RDP), a program based on the principles of political equality for each South African citizen and the unification of all South African provinces. As one of its first reform measures, the postapartheid government designed municipal budgets that would inevitably impose higher property taxes and utility costs on South African whites. This tax revenue would then be used to provide shantytowns with basic utilities and public services, including medical clinics and fire departments. Along with budget changes in 1994, the government issued a land reform bill that allows millions of South African blacks displaced from their native lands to reclaim ownership.

Since the installation of the interim coalition government, South Africa has made great cultural and economic advances. Postapartheid South Africa has seen the end of the United Nations' cultural boycott enacted in 1950 as well as of subsequent boycotts by British playwrights. Already, black artists are receiving international recognition for their paintings, sculptures, plays, and books. Film screenings in South Africa have steadily increased, and theater is thriving. Along with the staging of dramas written and acted by black Africans in established theaters such as the Market Theatre in Johannesburg, various types of experimental theater have emerged. Community theaters in particular are providing venues for plays centering on the local social issues. Even the South African Broadcasting Corporation has made plans for future multilingual programming.

Today, South Africa is beginning to recover from the economic downturn that plagued the 1980s. Democracy has restored much of the nation's appeal to foreign investors, and as a result, hundreds of foreign businesses and banks have returned to South Africa. Even though the rand, South Africa's basic unit of currency, has recently experienced some discouraging fluctuations, mineral and petroleum mining have continued to draw foreign investments and stimulate the South African economy.

In May of 1996, Mandela's government drafted South Africa's newest constitution, which is scheduled to be enacted in 1999. This new democratic constitution renounces racial discrimination and guarantees for all South Africans the personal freedoms of speech and assembly. In addition, the constitution guarantees fundamental services—such as food, health care, and housing—to all South Africans.

Mandela's government has waged a vigorous campaign to desegregate schools, which has led to prohibitions on discrimination based on language and religious affiliation. In addition, Mandela has initiated a housing program and has guaranteed free health care for all South African citizens. Still, tackling the results of almost forty years under apartheid is a monumental task, and reform demands massive government funding which further strains the South African economy.

As South Africa approaches the millennium, the government will be forced to address the social ills afflicting its citizens. Among the many effects of apartheid still ravaging South African society are violence, unemployment, homelessness, and disease. In 1995, South Africa's homicide rates were eight times higher than those in the United States. During the same year, the number of unemployed South Africans surpassed fifty percent, and more than eight million South Africans were homeless. Moreover, an estimated eighty percent of the population still live in extreme poverty. Overpopulated and dilapidated shantytowns and homelands have encouraged the epidemic spread of tuberculosis and AIDS. By the mid-1980s, tuberculosis had permeated communities of white and black Africans in both rural and urban areas. More recently, South African health officials have estimated the number of citizens with AIDS to be as high as 1.2 million.

Despite the remaining social problems, South Africans remain hopeful. Now that apartheid has ended, there is little chance that South Africans will allow white dominance to reemerge. The coalition government continues to make strides and to uphold the ideals of democracy. Shortly after the adoption of the 1996 constitution, F. W. de Klerk announced the National Party's withdrawal from the coalition government and his plans to refocus the National Party on the platform of family values. Explaining the nature of the National Party's secession from the coalition government, de Klerk hinted at South Africa's future, saying, "Our decision should be seen as an important step in the growing maturity and normalization of our young democracy." Soon thereafter, the last of the South African provinces, Kwa-Zulu/Natal, voted in its first nonracial elections, officially bringing an end to the era of apartheid.

WORKS CONSULTED

Apartheid. Paris: UNESCO, 1972.

Biko, Steve. "The Definition of Black Consciousness." *I Write What I Like: A Selection of Writings.* Ed. Aelred Stubbs. San Francisco: Harper, 1986. 48–53.

Callan, Edward. "Alan Paton and the Liberal Party." *The Long View.* Ed. Alan Paton. New York: Praeger, 1968. 1–10.

Dayley, Suzanne. "De Klerk's Party Quits Government." *New York Times* 10 May 1996, late ed.: A1.

———. "South Africa Losing Battle to House Homeless." *New York Times* 3 May 1996, late ed.: A1.

Internal Commission of Jurists. *South Africa: Human Rights and the Rule of Law.* Ed. Geoffrey Bindman. London: Pinter, 1988.

Keller, Bill. "Next for the New South Africa: Potholes and Taxes." *New York Times* 9 July 1994, late NY ed.: 3.

———. "A Post-Apartheid Nightmare: Hospitals Swamped." *New York Times* 29 Aug. 1994, late NY ed.: A4.

———. "Rival Visions of Freedom Split South African Zulus." *New York Times* 4 Apr. 1994, late NY ed.: A1.

Lawrence, John C. *Race Propaganda and South Africa.* London: Victor, 1979.

Marx, Anthony M. *Lessons of the Struggle: South African Internal Opposition, 1960–1990.* New York: Oxford, 1992.

McLarin, Kimberly J. "The Voice of Apartheid Goes Multicultural." *New York Times* 25 July 1995, late NY ed.: A2.

Ohlson, Thomas, and Stephen John Stedman, with Robert Davies. *The New Is Not Yet Born: Conflict Resolution in Southern Africa.* Washington: Brookings, 1994.

Omer-Cooper, J. D. *History of Southern Africa.* London: James Currey, 1987.

"South Africa Murders Soar." *New York Times* 18 Apr. 1996, late ed.: A10.

"South Africa's Muddle: Drift of the Beloved Country." *World Press Review* 42 (Jan. 1995): 8–14.

Thompson, Leonard. *A History of South Africa.* New Haven: Yale UP, 1990.

Wall, James M. "Tutu's Peace Protest Provides Ray of Hope." *Christian Century* 102 (17 Apr. 1985): 371–72

Whitaker, Mark. "Cry, the South African Writer." *Newsweek* 4 Aug. 1986: 29.

Literature

About the Author

ATHOL FUGARD (1932–) has gained a reputation as a world-renowned playwright, director, and actor. His plays, which Fugard himself has often directed and acted in, have been produced in his native South Africa, in London, and off-Broadway in New York. Fugard's plays have gained international recognition because of their poignant depictions of the human condition within the context of the South African landscape and culture. Thus, inherent in Fugard's plays are the personal consequences of living with and in the wake of apartheid. While Fugard's themes are more personal than political, his plays have generated some controversy about Fugard's political intentions. Although, as Fugard admits, "it is impossible to not be political in South Africa," he maintains that his role as author is the same as any other regional writer—he writes what he sees.

Born in the Karoo village of Middleburg, Athol Harold Lannagan Fugard grew up in Port Elizabeth, South Africa, with his father of Polish/Irish descent and his Afrikaner mother. In 1953, after two years at the University of Cape Town, Fugard traveled as a merchant seaman. Subsequently, he worked as a freelance journalist and as a clerk in the Native Commissioner's Court in Fordsburg, the pass law court. Fugard moved to London in 1959 to take part in the theater there. In 1962, having returned to Cape Town, he wrote a letter supporting the British playwrights' boycott of South African theater until audiences were unsegregated; as a result the South African government confiscated his passport and placed his family under state surveillance. Fugard then turned his attention to South African theater, aligning himself with the Serpent Players, a black acting company. In 1973, Fugard and his wife, Sheila, founded the Space Theatre, from which the Market Theatre evolved. By 1982, Fugard was producing his plays internationally. Today, Fugard and his family maintain one residence in Port Elizabeth and another in New Bethesda, South Africa. Along with writing, directing, and acting in his plays, Fugard often teaches university theater workshops and works with youth theaters in South Africa and the United States.

During the past forty years, Fugard has amassed a large canon of plays, including *The Blood Knot* (1964), *People Are Living There* (1963), *Hello and Goodbye* (1965), *Boesman and Lena* (1969), *Sizwe Bansi Is Dead* (1972), *The Island* (1973), *Statements after an Arrest under the Immorality Act* (1973), *A Lesson from Aloes* (1981), *The Road to Mecca* (1985), and *My Children! My Africa!* (1985). Fugard has also published one novel, *Tsotsi* (1960–61). With the end of apartheid, Fugard has begun to focus his plays on the themes of hope, courage, and change, all of which are present in his most recent play, *Valley Song* (1996).

"Master Harold" . . . *and the boys* (1982), first produced at the Yale Repertory Theatre, has been called one of Fugard's most successful plays. It is set in the year 1950, and the echoes of the Immorality Act and the Population Registration Act, instituted in that year, can be seen in the racial tension of the play. Perhaps even more important, however, are the more personal themes of acceptance and rejection, loyalty and friendship, and shame. Despite the play's focus on the emotional and personal rather than the political, the South African Directorate of Publications, for a short time, banned printed versions of the play. First published in the 1982 winter issue of Yale's *Theater*, *"Master Harold"* . . . *and the boys* has yet to be published in South Africa. The play did, however, premiere in Johannesburg, South Africa, in March 1983 before a multiracial audience including such notable South Africans as Nadine Gordimer and Bishop Desmond Tutu.

Significantly, Fugard has admitted that *"Master Harold"* . . . *and the boys* is his most autobiographical work. The autobiographical incident on which the play is based is recounted in his *Notebooks 1960–1977* (1983); excerpts from this account can be found on pages 101–103.

ATHOL FUGARD

"Master Harold" . . . and the boys
(1982)

*The St. George's Park Tea Room on a wet and windy Port Elizabeth[1]
afternoon.*

*Tables and chairs have been cleared and are stacked on one side except for
one which stands apart with a single chair. On this table a knife, fork, spoon and
side plate in anticipation of a simple meal, together with a pile of comic books.*

*Other elements: a serving counter with a few stale cakes under glass and a
not very impressive display of sweets, cigarettes and cool drinks, etc.; a few cardboard advertising handouts — Cadbury's Chocolate, Coca-Cola — and a black-
board on which an untrained hand has chalked up the prices of Tea, Coffee,
Scones, Milkshakes — all flavors — and Cool Drinks; a few sad ferns in pots; a
telephone; an old-style jukebox.*

There is an entrance on one side and an exit into a kitchen on the other.

*Leaning on the solitary table, his head cupped in one hand as he pages
through one of the comic books, is Sam. A black man in his mid-forties. He wears
the white coat of a waiter. Behind him on his knees, mopping down the floor
with a bucket of water and a rag, is Willie. Also black and about the same age as
Sam. He has his sleeves and trousers rolled up.*

The year: 1950

1   WILLIE: [*Singing as he works.*]
         "She was scandalizin' my name,
         She took my money
         She called me honey
         But she was scandalizin' my name.
         Called it love but was playin' a game . . ."

---

[1]   city on the southeast coast of South Africa

He gets up and moves the bucket. Stands thinking for a moment, then, raising his arms to hold an imaginary partner, he launches into an intricate ballroom dance step. Although a mildly comic figure, he reveals a reasonable degree of accomplishment.

Hey, Sam.

Sam, absorbed in the comic book, does not respond.

Hey, Boet Sam!

Sam looks up.

I'm getting it. The quickstep. Look now and tell me. [*He repeats the step.*] Well?

SAM: [*Encouragingly.*] Show me again.

WILLIE: Okay, count for me.

SAM: Ready?

5   WILLIE: Ready.

SAM: Five, six, seven, eight . . . [*Willie starts to dance.*] A-n-d one two three four . . . and one two three four. . . . [*Ad libbing as Willie dances.*] Your shoulders, Willie . . . your shoulders! Don't look down! Look happy, Willie! Relax, Willie!

WILLIE: [*Desperate but still dancing.*] I am relax.

SAM: No, you're not.

WILLIE: [*He falters.*] Ag no man, Sam! Mustn't talk. You make me make mistakes.

10   SAM: But you're too stiff.

WILLIE: Yesterday I'm not straight . . . today I'm too stiff!

SAM: Well, you are. You asked me and I'm telling you.

WILLIE: Where?

SAM: Everywhere. Try to glide through it.

15   WILLIE: Glide?

SAM: Ja, make it smooth. And give it more style. It must look like you're enjoying yourself.

WILLIE: [*Emphatically.*] I wasn't.

SAM: Exactly.

WILLIE: How can I enjoy myself? Not straight, too stiff and now it's also glide, give it more style, make it smooth. . . . Haai! Is hard to remember all those things, Boet Sam.

20   SAM: That's your trouble. You're trying too hard.

WILLIE: I try hard because it *is* hard.

SAM: But don't let me see it. The secret is to make it look easy. Ballroom must look happy, Willie, not like hard work. It must . . . Ja! . . . it must look like romance.

WILLIE: Now another one! What's romance?

SAM: Love story with happy ending. A handsome man in tails, and in his arms, smiling at him, a beautiful lady in evening dress!

25   WILLIE: Fred Astaire, Ginger Rogers.

SAM: You got it. Tapdance or ballroom, it's the same. Romance. In two weeks' time when the judges look at you and Hilda, they must see a man and a woman who are dancing their way to a happy ending. What I saw was you holding her like you were frightened she was going to run away.

WILLIE: Ja! Because that is what she wants to do! I got no romance left for Hilda anymore, Boet Sam.

SAM: Then pretend. When you put your arms around Hilda, imagine she is Ginger Rogers.

WILLIE: With no teeth? You try.

30   SAM: Well, just remember, there's only two weeks left.

WILLIE: I know, I know! [*To the jukebox.*] I do it better with music. You got sixpence for Sarah Vaughan?[2]

SAM: That's a slow foxtrot. You're practicing the quickstep.

WILLIE: I'll practice slow foxtrot.

SAM: [*Shaking his head.*] It's your turn to put money in the jukebox.

35   WILLIE: I only got bus fare to go home. [*He returns disconsolately to his work.*] Love story and happy ending! She's doing it all right, Boet Sam, but is not me she's giving happy endings. Fuckin' whore! Three nights now she doesn't come practice. I wind up gramophone, I get record ready and I sit and wait. What happens? Nothing. Ten o'clock I start dancing with my pillow. You try and practice romance by yourself, Boet Sam. Struesgod, she doesn't come tonight I take back my dress and ballroom shoes and I find me new partner. Size twenty-six. Shoes size seven. And now she's also making trouble for me with the baby again. Reports me to Child Wellfed, that I'm not giving her money. She lies! Every week I am giving her money for milk. And how do I

---

2   Sarah Vaughan (1924–1990)—U.S. jazz and blues singer

know is my baby? Only his hair looks like me. She's fucking
around all the time I turn my back. Hilda Samuels is a bitch!
[*Pause.*] Hey, Sam!

SAM: Ja.

WILLIE: You listening?

SAM: Ja.

WILLIE: So what you say?

40 SAM: About Hilda?

WILLIE: Ja.

SAM: When did you last give her a hiding?

WILLIE: [*Reluctantly.*] Sunday night.

SAM: And today is Thursday.

45 WILLIE: [*He knows what's coming.*] Okay.

SAM: Hiding on Sunday night, then Monday, Tuesday and Wednes-
day she doesn't come to practice . . . and you are asking me why?

WILLIE: I said okay, Boet Sam!

SAM: You hit her too much. One day she's going to leave you for
good.

WILLIE: So? She makes me the hell-in too much.

50 SAM: [*Emphasizing his point.*] *Too* much and *too* hard. You had the
same trouble with Eunice.

WILLIE: Because she also make the hell-in, Boet Sam. She never got
the steps right. Even the waltz.

SAM: Beating her up every time she makes a mistake in the waltz?
[*Shaking his head.*] No, Willie! That takes the pleasure out of
ballroom dancing.

WILLIE: Hilda is not too bad with the waltz, Boet Sam. Is the quickstep where the trouble starts.

SAM: [*Teasing him gently.*] How's your pillow with the quickstep?

55 WILLIE: [*Ignoring the tease.*] Good! And why? Because it got no legs.
That's her trouble. She can't move them quick enough, Boet Sam.
I start the record and before halfway Count Basie [3] is already winning. Only time we catch up with him is when gramophone runs
down.

Sam laughs.

---

[3] William "Count" Basie (1904–1984)—U.S. jazz pianist, composer, and bandleader

Haaikona, Boet Sam, is not funny.

SAM: [*Snapping his fingers.*] I got it! Give her a handicap.

WILLIE: What's that?

SAM: Give her a ten-second start and then let Count Basie go. Then I put my money on her. Hot favorite in the Ballroom Stakes: Hilda Samuels ridden by Willie Malopo.

WILLIE: [*Turning away.*] I'm not talking to you no more.

60 SAM: [*Relenting.*] Sorry, Willie . . .

WILLIE: It's finish between us.

SAM: Okay, okay . . . I'll stop.

WILLIE: You can also fuck off.

SAM: Willie, listen! I want to help you!

65 WILLIE: No more jokes?

SAM: I promise.

WILLIE: Okay. Help me.

SAM: [*His turn to hold an imaginary partner.*] Look and learn. Feet together. Back straight. Body relaxed. Right hand placed gently in the small of her back and wait for the music. Don't start worrying about making mistakes or the judges or the other competitors. It's just you, Hilda and the music, and you're going to have a good time. What Count Basie do you play?

WILLIE: "You the cream in my coffee, you the salt in my stew."

70 SAM: Right. Give it to me in strict tempo.

WILLIE: Ready?

SAM: Ready.

WILLIE: A-n-d . . . [*Singing.*]
"You the cream in my coffee.
You the salt in my stew.
You will always be my
necessity.
I'd be lost without
you. . . ." [*etc.*]

Sam launches into the quickstep. He is obviously a much more accomplished dancer than Willie. Hally enters. A seventeen-year-old white boy. Wet raincoat and school case. He stops and watches Sam. The demonstration comes to an end with a flourish. Applause from Hally and Willie.

HALLY: Bravo! No question about it. First place goes to Mr. Sam Semela.

75 WILLIE: [*In total agreement.*] You was gliding with style, Boet Sam.

HALLY: [*Cheerfully.*] How's it, chaps?

SAM: Okay, Hally.

WILLIE: [*Springing to attention like a soldier and saluting.*] At your service, Master Harold!

HALLY: Not long to the big event, hey!

80 SAM: Two weeks.

HALLY: You nervous?

SAM: No.

HALLY: Think you stand a chance?

SAM: Let's just say I'm ready to go out there and dance.

85 HALLY: It looked like it. What about you, Willie?

Willie groans.

What's the matter?

SAM: He's got leg trouble.

HALLY: [*Innocently.*] Oh, sorry to hear that, Willie.

WILLIE: Boet Sam! You promised. [*Willie returns to his work.*]

Hally deposits his school case and takes off his raincoat. His clothes are a little neglected and untidy: black blazer with school badge, gray flannel trousers in need of an ironing, khaki shirt and tie, black shoes. Sam has fetched a towel for Hally to dry his hair.

HALLY: God, what a lousy bloody day. It's coming down cats and dogs out there. Bad for business, chaps . . . [*Conspiratorial whisper.*] . . . but it also means we're in for a nice quiet afternoon.

90 SAM: You can speak loud. Your Mom's not here.

HALLY: Out shopping?

SAM: No. The hospital.

HALLY: But it's Thursday. There's no visiting on Thursday afternoons. Is my Dad okay?

SAM: Sounds like it. In fact, I think he's going home.

95 HALLY: [*Stopped short by Sam's remark.*] What do you mean?

SAM: The hospital phoned.

HALLY: To say what?

SAM: I don't know. I just heard your Mom talking.

HALLY: So what makes you say he's going home?

100 SAM: It sounded as if they were telling her to come and fetch him.

Hally thinks about what Sam has said for a few seconds.

HALLY: When did she leave?
SAM: About an hour ago. She said she would phone you. Want
to eat?

Hally doesn't respond.

Hally, want your lunch?
HALLY: I suppose so. [*His mood has changed.*] What's on the menu? . . .
as if I don't know.
SAM: Soup, followed by meat pie and gravy.
105 HALLY: Today's?
SAM: No.
HALLY: And the soup?
SAM: Nourishing pea soup.
HALLY: Just the soup. [*The pile of comic books on the table.*] And these?
110 SAM: For your Dad. Mr. Kempston brought them.
HALLY: You haven't been reading them, have you?
SAM: Just looking.
HALLY: [*Examining the comics.*] *Jungle Jim* . . . *Batman and Robin* . . .
Tarzan . . . God, what rubbish! Mental pollution. Take them
away.

Sam exits waltzing into the kitchen. Hally turns to Willie.

HALLY: Did you hear my Mom talking on the telephone, Willie?
115 WILLIE: No, Master Hally. I was at the back.
HALLY: And she didn't say anything to you before she left?
WILLIE: She said I must clean the floors.
HALLY: I mean about my Dad.
WILLIE: She didn't say nothing to me about him, Master Hally.
120 HALLY: [*With conviction.*] No! It can't be. They said he needed at
least another three weeks of treatment. Sam's definitely made a
mistake. [*Rummages through his school case, finds a book and settles
down at the table to read.*] So, Willie!
WILLIE: Yes, Master Hally! Schooling okay today?
HALLY: Yes, okay. . . . [*He thinks about it.*] . . . No, not really. Ag,
what's the difference? I don't care. And Sam says you've got
problems.

WILLIE: Big problems.

HALLY: Which leg is sore?

Willie groans.

> Both legs.

125   WILLIE: There is nothing wrong with my legs. Sam is just making jokes.

HALLY: So then you *will* be in the competition.

WILLIE: Only if I can find me a partner.

HALLY: But what about Hilda?

SAM: [*Returning with a bowl of soup.*] She's the one who's got trouble with her legs.

130   HALLY: What sort of trouble, Willie?

SAM: From the way he describes it, I think the lady has gone a bit lame.

HALLY: Good God! Have you taken her to see a doctor?

SAM: I think a vet would be better.

HALLY: What do you mean?

135   SAM: What do you call it again when a racehorse goes very fast?

HALLY: Gallop?

SAM: That's it!

WILLIE: Boet Sam!

HALLY: "A gallop down the homestretch to the winning post." But what's that got to do with Hilda?

140   SAM: Count Basie always gets there first.

Willie lets fly with his slop rag. It misses Sam and hits Hally.

> HALLY: [*Furious.*] For Christ's sake, Willie! What the hell do you think you're doing!

WILLIE: Sorry, Master Hally, but it's him. . . .

HALLY: Act your bloody age! [*Hurls the rag back at Willie.*] Cut out the nonsense now and get on with your work. And you too, Sam. Stop fooling around.

Sam moves away.

> No. Hang on. I haven't finished! Tell me exactly what my Mom said.

SAM: I have. "When Hally comes, tell him I've gone to the hospital and I'll phone him."

145   HALLY: She didn't say anything about taking my Dad home?

SAM: No. It's just that when she was talking on the phone . . .

HALLY: [*Interrupting him.*] No, Sam. They can't be discharging him. She would have said so if they were. In any case, we saw him last night and he wasn't in good shape at all. Staff nurse even said there was talk about taking more X-rays. And now suddenly today he's better? If anything, it sounds more like a bad turn to me . . . which I sincerely hope it isn't. Hang on . . . how long ago did you say she left?

SAM: Just before two . . . [*His wrist watch.*] . . . hour and a half.

HALLY: I know how to settle it. [*Behind the counter to the telephone. Talking as he dials.*] Let's give her ten minutes to get to the hospital, ten minutes to load him up, another ten, at the most, to get home and another ten to get him inside. Forty minutes. They should have been home for at least half an hour already. [*Pause— he waits with the receiver to his ear.*] No reply, chaps. And you know why? Because she's at his bedside in hospital helping him pull through a bad turn. You definitely heard wrong.

150   SAM: Okay.

As far as Hally is concerned, the matter is settled. He returns to his table, sits down and divides his attention between the book and his soup. Sam is at his school case and picks up a textbook, Modern Graded Mathematics for Standards Nine and Ten. *Opens it at random and laughs at something he sees.*

Who is this supposed to be?

HALLY: Old fart-face Prentice.

SAM: Teacher?

HALLY: Thinks he is. And believe me, that is not a bad likeness.

SAM: Has he seen it?

155   HALLY: Yes.

SAM: What did he say?

HALLY: Tried to be clever, as usual. Said I was no Leonardo da Vinci and that bad art had to be punished. So, six of the best, and his are bloody good.

SAM: On your bum?

HALLY: Where else? The days when I got them on my hands are gone forever, Sam.

160 SAM: With your trousers down!

HALLY: No. He's not quite that barbaric.

SAM: That's the way they do it in jail.

HALLY: [*Flicker of morbid interest.*] Really?

SAM: Ja. When the magistrate sentences you to "strokes with a light cane."

165 HALLY: Go on.

SAM: They make you lie down on a bench. One policeman pulls down your trousers and holds your ankles, another one pulls your shirt over your head and holds your arms . . .

HALLY: Thank you! That's enough.

SAM: . . . and the one that gives you the strokes talks to you gently and for a long time between each one. [*He laughs.*]

HALLY: I've heard enough, Sam! Jesus! It's a bloody awful world when you come to think of it. People can be real bastards.

170 SAM: That's the way it is, Hally.

HALLY: It doesn't *have* to be that way. There is something called progress, you know. We don't exactly burn people at the stake anymore.

SAM: Like Joan of Arc.

HALLY: Correct. If she was captured today, she'd be given a fair trial.

SAM: And then the death sentence.

175 HALLY: [*A world-weary sigh.*] I know, I know! I oscillate between hope and despair for this world as well, Sam. But things will change, you wait and see. One day somebody is going to get up and give history a kick up the backside and get it going again.

SAM: Like who?

HALLY: [*After thought.*] They're called social reformers. Every age, Sam, has got its social reformer. My history book is full of them.

SAM: So where's ours?

HALLY: Good question. And I hate to say it, but the answer is: I don't know. Maybe he hasn't even been born yet. Or is still only a babe in arms at his mother's breast. God, what a thought.

180 SAM: So we just go on waiting.

HALLY: Ja, looks like it. [*Back to his soup and the book.*]

SAM: [*Reading from the textbook.*] "Introduction: In some mathematical problems only the magnitude . . ." [*He mispronounces the word "magnitude."*]

HALLY: [*Correcting him without looking up.*] Magnitude.

SAM: What's it mean?

185   HALLY: How big it is. The size of the thing.

SAM: [*Reading.*] ". . . a magnitude of the quantities is of importance. In other problems we need to know whether these quantities are negative or positive. For example, whether there is a debit or credit bank balance . . ."

HALLY: Whether you're broke or not.

SAM: ". . . whether the temperature is above or below Zero . . ."

HALLY: Naught degrees. Cheerful state of affairs! No cash and you're freezing to death. Mathematics won't get you out of that one.

190   SAM: "All these quantities are called . . ." [*Spelling the word.*] . . . s-c-a-l . . .

HALLY: Scalars.

SAM: Scalars! [*Shaking his head with a laugh.*] You understand all that?

HALLY: [*Turning a page.*] No. And I don't intend to try.

SAM: So what happens when the exams come?

195   HALLY: Failing a maths exam isn't the end of the world, Sam. How many times have I told you that examination results don't measure intelligence?

SAM: I would say about as many times as you've failed one of them.

HALLY: [*Mirthlessly.*] Ha, ha, ha.

SAM: [*Simultaneously.*] Ha, ha, ha.

HALLY: Just remember Winston Churchill didn't do particularly well at school.

200   SAM: You've also told me that one many times.

HALLY: Well, it just so happens to be the truth.

SAM: [*Enjoying the word.*] Magnitude! Magnitude! Show me how to use it.

HALLY: [*After thought.*] An intrepid social reformer will not be daunted by the magnitude of the task he has undertaken.

SAM: [*Impressed.*] Couple of jaw-breakers in there!

205   HALLY: I gave you three for the price of one. Intrepid, daunted and magnitude. I did that once in an exam. Put five of the words I had to explain in one sentence. It was half a page long.

SAM: Well, I'll put my money on you in the English exam.

HALLY: Piece of cake. Eighty percent without even trying.

SAM: [*Another textbook from Hally's case.*] And history?

HALLY: So-so. I'll scrape through. In the fifties if I'm lucky.

210   SAM: You didn't do too badly last year.

HALLY: Because we had World War One. That at least had some action. You try to find that in the South African Parliamentary system.

SAM: [*Reading from the history textbook.*] "Napoleon and the principle of equality." Hey! This sounds interesting. "After concluding peace with Britain in 1802, Napoleon used a brief period of calm to in-sti-tute . . ."

HALLY: Introduce.

SAM: ". . . many reforms. Napoleon regarded all people as equal before the law and wanted them to have equal opportunities for advancement. All ves-ti-ges of the feu-dal system with its oppression of the poor were abolished." Vestiges, feudal system and abolished. I'm all right on oppression.

215 HALLY: I'm thinking. He swept away . . . abolished . . . the last remains . . . vestiges . . . of the bad old days . . . feudal system.

SAM: Ha! There's the social reformer we're waiting for. He sounds like a man of some magnitude.

HALLY: I'm not so sure about that. It's a damn good title for a book, though. A man of magnitude!

SAM: He sounds pretty big to me, Hally.

HALLY: Don't confuse historical significance with greatness. But maybe I'm being a bit prejudiced. Have a look in there and you'll see he's two chapters long. And hell! . . . has he only got dates, Sam, all of which you've got to remember! This campaign and that campaign, and then, because of all the fighting, the next thing is we get Peace Treaties all over the place. And what's the end of the story? Battle of Waterloo, which he loses. Wasn't worth it. No, I don't know about him as a man of magnitude.

220 SAM: Then who would you say was?

HALLY: To answer that, we need a definition of greatness, and I suppose that would be somebody who . . . somebody who benefited all mankind.

SAM: Right. But like who?

HALLY: [*He speaks with total conviction.*] Charles Darwin. Remember him? That big book from the library. *The Origin of the Species.*

SAM: Him?

225 HALLY: Yes. For his Theory of Evolution.

SAM: You didn't finish it.

HALLY: I ran out of time. I didn't finish it because my two weeks was up. But I'm going to take it out again after I've digested what I read. It's safe. I've hidden it away in the Theology section. Nobody ever goes in there. And anyway who are you to talk? You hardly even looked at it.

SAM: I tried. I looked at the chapters in the beginning and I saw one called "The Struggle for an Existence." Ah ha, I thought. At last! But what did I get? Something called the mistletoe which needs the apple tree and there's too many seeds and all are going to die except one . . . ! No, Hally.

HALLY: [*Intellectually outraged.*] What do you mean, No! The poor man had to start somewhere. For God's sake, Sam, he revolutionized science. Now we know.

230   SAM: What?

HALLY: Where we come from and what it all means.

SAM: And that's a benefit to mankind? Anyway, I still don't believe it.

HALLY: God, you're impossible. I showed it to you in black and white.

SAM: Doesn't mean I got to believe it.

235   HALLY: It's the likes of you that kept the Inquisition in business. It's called bigotry. Anyway, that's my man of magnitude. Charles Darwin! Who's yours?

SAM: [*Without hesitation.*] Abraham Lincoln.

HALLY: I might have guessed as much. Don't get sentimental, Sam. You've never been a slave, you know. And anyway we freed your ancestors here in South Africa long before the Americans. But if you want to thank somebody on their behalf, do it to Mr. William Wilberforce.⁴ Come on. Try again. I want a real genius. [*Now enjoying himself, and so is Sam. Hally goes behind the counter and helps himself to a chocolate.*]

SAM: William Shakespeare.

HALLY: [*No enthusiasm.*] Oh. So you're also one of them, are you? You're basing that opinion on only one play, you know. You've only read my *Julius Caesar* and even I don't understand half of what they're talking about. They should do what they did with the old Bible: bring the language up to date.

240   SAM: That's all you've got. It's also the only one *you've* read.

---

⁴ William Wilberforce (1759–1833)—English abolitionist

HALLY: I know. I admit it. That's why I suggest we reserve our judgment until we've checked up on a few others. I've got a feeling, though, that by the end of this year one is going to be enough for me, and I can give you the names of twenty-nine other chaps in the Standard Nine class of the Port Elizabeth Technical College who feel the same. But if you want him, you can have him. My turn now. [*Pacing.*] This is a damned good exercise, you know! It started off looking like a simple question and here it's got us really probing into the intellectual heritage of our civilization.

SAM: So who is it going to be?

HALLY: My next man . . . and he gets the title on two scores: social reform and literary genius . . . is Leo Nikolaevich Tolstoy.

SAM: That Russian.

245 HALLY: Correct. Remember the picture of him I showed you?

SAM: With the long beard.

HALLY: [*Trying to look like Tolstoy.*] And those burning, visionary eyes. My God, the face of a social prophet if ever I saw one! And remember my words when I showed it to you? Here's a *man,* Sam!

SAM: Those were words, Hally.

HALLY: Not many intellectuals are prepared to shovel manure with the peasants and then go home and write a "little book" called *War and Peace.* Incidentally, Sam, he was somebody else who, to quote, ". . . did not distinguish himself scholastically."

250 SAM: Meaning?

HALLY: He was also no good at school.

SAM: Like you and Winston Churchill.

HALLY: [*Mirthlessly.*] Ha, ha, ha.

SAM: [*Simultaneously.*] Ha, ha, ha.

255 HALLY: Don't get clever, Sam. That man freed his serfs of his own free will.

SAM: No argument. He was a somebody, all right. I accept him.

HALLY: I'm sure Count Tolstoy will be very pleased to hear that. Your turn. Shoot. [*Another chocolate from behind the counter.*] I'm waiting, Sam.

SAM: I've got him.

HALLY: Good. Submit your candidate for examination.

260 SAM: Jesus.

HALLY: [*Stopped dead in his tracks.*] Who?

SAM: Jesus Christ.

HALLY: Oh, come on, Sam!

SAM: The Messiah.

265 HALLY: Ja, but still . . . No, Sam. Don't let's get started on religion. We'll just spend the whole afternoon arguing again. Suppose I turn around and say Mohammed?

SAM: All right.

HALLY: You can't have them both on the same list!

SAM: Why not? You like Mohammed, I like Jesus.

HALLY: I *don't* like Mohammed. I never have. I was merely being hypothetical. As far as I'm concerned, the Koran is as bad as the Bible. No. Religion is out! I'm not going to waste my time again arguing with you about the existence of God. You know perfectly well I'm an atheist . . . and I've got homework to do.

270 SAM: Okay, I take him back.

HALLY: You've got time for one more name.

SAM: [*After thought.*] I've got one I know we'll agree on. A simple straightforward great Man of Magnitude . . . and no arguments. And *he* really *did* benefit all mankind.

HALLY: I wonder. After your last contribution I'm beginning to doubt whether anything in the way of an intellectual agreement is possible between the two of us. Who is he?

SAM: Guess.

275 HALLY: Socrates? Alexandre Dumas? Karl Marx? Dostoevsky? Nietzsche?

Sam shakes his head after each name.

Give me a clue.

SAM: The letter P is important . . .

HALLY: Plato!

SAM: . . . and his name begins with an F.

HALLY: I've got it. Freud and Psychology.

280 SAM: No. I didn't understand him.

HALLY: That makes two of us.

SAM: Think of mouldy apricot jam.

HALLY: [*After a delighted laugh.*] Penicillin and Sir Alexander Fleming! And the title of the book: *The Microbe Hunters.* [*Delighted.*] Splendid, Sam! Splendid. For once we are in total agreement. The major breakthrough in medical science in the Twentieth Century. If it wasn't for him, we might have lost the Second World

War. It's deeply gratifying, Sam, to know that I haven't been wasting my time in talking to you. [*Strutting around proudly.*] Tolstoy may have educated his peasants, but I've educated you.

SAM: Standard Four to Standard Nine.

285 HALLY: Have we been at it as long as that?

SAM: Yep. And my first lesson was geography.

HALLY: [*Intrigued.*] Really? I don't remember.

SAM: My room there at the back of the old Jubilee Boarding House. I had just started working for your Mom. Little boy in short trousers walks in one afternoon and asks me seriously: "Sam, do you want to see South Africa?" Hey man! Sure I wanted to see South Africa!

HALLY: Was that me?

290 SAM: . . . So the next thing I'm looking at a map you had just done for homework. It was your first one and you were very proud of yourself.

HALLY: Go on.

SAM: Then came my first lesson. "Repeat after me, Sam: Gold in the Transvaal, mealies in the Free State, sugar in Natal and grapes in the Cape." I still know it!

HALLY: Well, I'll be buggered. So that's how it all started.

SAM: And your next map was one with all the rivers and the mountains they came from. The Orange, the Vaal, the Limpopo, the Zambezi . . .

295 HALLY: You've got a phenomenal memory!

SAM: You should be grateful. That is why you started passing your exams. You tried to be better than me.

They laugh together. Willie is attracted by the laughter and joins them.

HALLY: The old Jubilee Boarding House. Sixteen rooms with board and lodging, rent in advance and one week's notice. I haven't thought about it for donkey's years . . . and I don't think that's an accident. God, was I glad when we sold it and moved out. Those years are not remembered as the happiest ones of an unhappy childhood.

WILLIE: [*Knocking on the table and trying to imitate a woman's voice.*] "Hally, are you there?"

HALLY: Who's that supposed to be?

300 WILLIE: "What you doing in there, Hally? Come out at once!"

HALLY: [*To Sam.*] What's he talking about?

SAM: Don't you remember?

WILLIE: "Sam, Willie . . . is he in there with you boys?"

SAM: Hiding away in our room when your mother was looking for you.

305 HALLY: [*Another good laugh.*] Of course! I used to crawl and hide under your bed! But finish the story, Willie. Then what used to happen? You chaps would give the game away by telling her I was in there with you. So much for friendship.

SAM: We couldn't lie to her. She knew.

HALLY: Which meant I got another rowing for hanging around the "servants' quarters." I think I spent more time in there with you chaps than anywhere else in that dump. And do you blame me? Nothing but bloody misery wherever you went. Somebody was always complaining about the food, or my mother was having a fight with Micky Nash because she'd caught her with a petty officer in her room. Maud Meiring was another one. Remember those two? They were prostitutes, you know. Soldiers and sailors from the troopships. Bottom fell out of the business when the war ended. God, the flotsam and jetsam that life washed up on our shores! No joking, if it wasn't for your room, I would have been the first certified ten-year-old in medical history. Ja, the memories are coming back now. Walking home from school and thinking: "What can I do this afternoon?" Try out a few ideas, but sooner or later I'd end up in there with you fellows. I bet you I could still find my way to your room with my eyes closed. [*He does exactly that.*] Down the corridor . . . telephone on the right, which my Mom keeps locked because somebody is using it on the sly and not paying . . . past the kitchen and unappetizing cooking smells . . . around the corner into the backyard, hold my breath again because there are more smells coming when I pass your lavatory, then into that little passageway, first door on the right and into your room. How's that?

SAM: Good. But, as usual, you forgot to knock.

HALLY: Like that time I barged in and caught you and Cynthia . . . at it. Remember? God, was I embarrassed! I didn't know what was going on at first.

310 SAM: Ja, that taught you a lesson.

HALLY: And about a lot more than knocking on doors, I'll have you know, and I don't mean geography either. Hell, Sam, couldn't you have waited until it was dark?

SAM: No.

HALLY: Was it that urgent?

SAM: Yes, and if you don't believe me, wait until your time comes.

315 HALLY: No, thank you. I am not interested in girls. [*Back to his memories . . . Using a few chairs he recreates the room as he lists the items.*] A gray little room with a cold cement floor. Your bed against that wall . . . and I now know why the mattress sags so much! . . . Willie's bed . . . it's propped up on bricks because one leg is broken . . . that wobbly little table with the washbasin and jug of water . . . Yes! . . . stuck to the wall above it are some pin-up pictures from magazines. Joe Louis . . .

WILLIE: Brown Bomber. World Title. [*Boxing pose.*] Three rounds and knockout.[5]

HALLY: Against who?

SAM: Max Schmeling.

HALLY: Correct. I can also remember Fred Astaire and Ginger Rogers, and Rita Hayworth in a bathing costume which always made me hot and bothered when I looked at it. Under Willie's bed is an old suitcase with all his clothes in a mess, which is why I never hide there. Your things are neat and tidy in a trunk next to your bed, and on it there is a picture of you and Cynthia in your ballroom clothes, your first silver cup for third place in a competition and an old radio which doesn't work anymore. Have I left out anything?

320 SAM: No.

HALLY: Right, so much for the stage directions. Now the characters. [*Sam and Willie move to their appropriate positions in the bedroom.*] Willie is in bed, under his blankets with his clothes on, complaining nonstop about something, but we can't make out a word of what he's saying because he's got his head under the blankets as well. You're on your bed trimming your toenails with a knife— not a very edifying sight—and as for me . . . What am I doing?

SAM: You're sitting on the floor giving Willie a lecture about being a good loser while you get the checker board and pieces ready for a

---

[5] In 1938, U.S. boxer Joe Louis (Joseph Louis Barrows: 1914–1981), the "Brown Bomber," reclaimed the heavyweight title from German Max Schmeling (1905–   ) by a decisive knockout. Schmeling had won the title from Louis in 1936. Because of the rise of Nazism and Hitler's well-known disdain for so-called impure races, Louis's victory was highly symbolic.

game. Then you go to Willie's bed, pull off the blankets and make him play with you first because you know you're going to win, and that gives you the second game with me.

HALLY: And you certainly were a bad loser, Willie!

WILLIE: Haai!

325 HALLY: Wasn't he, Sam? And so slow! A game with you almost took the whole afternoon. Thank God I gave up trying to teach you how to play chess.

WILLIE: You and Sam cheated.

HALLY: I never saw Sam cheat, and mine were mostly the mistakes of youth.

WILLIE: Then how is it you two was always winning?

HALLY: Have you ever considered the possibility, Willie, that it was because we were better than you?

330 WILLIE: Every time better?

HALLY: Not every time. There were occasions when we deliberately let you win a game so that you would stop sulking and go on playing with us. Sam used to wink at me when you weren't looking to show me it was time to let you win.

WILLIE: So then you two didn't play fair.

HALLY: It was for your benefit, Mr. Malopo, which is more than being fair. It was an act of self-sacrifice. [*To Sam.*] But you know what my best memory is, don't you?

SAM: No.

335 HALLY: Come on, guess. If your memory is so good, you must remember it as well.

SAM: We got up to a lot of tricks in there, Hally.

HALLY: This one was special, Sam.

SAM: I'm listening.

HALLY: It started off looking like another of those useless nothing-to-do afternoons. I'd already been down to Main Street looking for adventure, but nothing had happened. I didn't feel like climbing trees in the Donkin Park or pretending I was a private eye and following a stranger . . . so as usual: See what's cooking in Sam's room. This time it was you on the floor. You had two thin pieces of wood and you were smoothing them down with a knife. It didn't look particularly interesting, but when I asked you what you were doing, you just said, "Wait and see, Hally. Wait . . . and see" . . . in that secret sort of way of yours, so I knew there was a surprise coming. You teased me, you bugger, by being deliberately slow and not answering my questions!

Sam laughs.

> And whistling while you worked away! God, it was infuriating! I could have brained you! It was only when you tied them together in a cross and put that down on the brown paper that I realized what you were doing. "Sam is making a kite?" And when I asked you and you said "Yes" . . . ! [*Shaking his head with disbelief.*] The sheer audacity of it took my breath away. I mean, seriously, what the hell does a black man know about flying a kite? I'll be honest with you, Sam, I had no hopes for it. If you think I was excited and happy, you got another guess coming. In fact, I was shit-scared that we were going to make fools of ourselves. When we left the boarding house to go up onto the hill, I was praying quietly that there wouldn't be any other kids around to laugh at us.

340 SAM: [*Enjoying the memory as much as Hally.*] Ja, I could see that.

HALLY: I made it obvious, did I?

SAM: Ja. You refused to carry it.

HALLY: Do you blame me? Can you remember what the poor thing looked like? Tomato-box wood and brown paper! Flour and water for glue! Two of my mother's old stockings for a tail, and then all those bits and pieces of string you made me tie together so that we could fly it! Hell, no, that was now only asking for a miracle to happen.

SAM: Then the big argument when I told you to hold the string and run with it when I let go.

345 HALLY: I was prepared to run, all right, but straight back to the boarding house.

SAM: [*Knowing what's coming.*] So what happened?

HALLY: Come on, Sam, you remember as well as I do.

SAM: I want to hear it from you.

Hally pauses. He wants to be as accurate as possible.

> HALLY: You went a little distance from me down the hill, you held it up ready to let it go. . . . "This is it," I thought. "Like everything else in my life, here comes another fiasco." Then you shouted, "Go, Hally!" and I started to run. [*Another pause.*] I don't know how to describe it, Sam. Ja! The miracle happened! I was running, waiting for it to crash to the ground, but instead suddenly there was something alive behind me at the end of the string, tugging at it as if it wanted to be free. I looked back . . . [*Shakes*

his head.] . . . I still can't believe my eyes. It was flying! Looping around and trying to climb even higher into the sky. You shouted to me to let it have more string. I did, until there was none left and I was just holding that piece of wood we had tied it to. You came up and joined me. You were laughing.

350 SAM: So were you. And shouting, "It works, Sam! We've done it!"

HALLY: And we had! I was so proud of us! It was the most splendid thing I had ever seen. I wished there were hundreds of kids around to watch us. The part that scared me, though, was when you showed me how to make it dive down to the ground and then just when it was on the point of crashing, swoop up again!

SAM: You didn't want to try yourself.

HALLY: Of course not! I would have been suicidal if anything had happened to it. Watching you do it made me nervous enough. I was quite happy just to see it up there with its tail fluttering behind it. You left me after that, didn't you? You explained how to get it down, we tied it to the bench so that I could sit and watch it, and you went away. I wanted you to stay, you know. I was a little scared of having to look after it by myself.

SAM: [*Quietly.*] I had work to do, Hally.

355 HALLY: It was sort of sad bringing it down, Sam. And it looked sad again when it was lying there on the ground. Like something that had lost its soul. Just tomato-box wood, brown paper and two of my mother's old stockings! But hell, I'll never forget that first moment when I saw it up there. I had a stiff neck the next day from looking up so much.

Sam laughs. Hally turns to him with a question he never thought of asking before.

Why did you make that kite, Sam?

SAM: [*Evenly.*] I can't remember.

HALLY: Truly?

SAM: Too long ago, Hally.

HALLY: Ja, I suppose it was. It's time for another one, you know.

360 SAM: Why do you say that?

HALLY: Because it feels like that. Wouldn't be a good day to fly it, though.

SAM: No. You can't fly kites on rainy days.

HALLY: [*He studies Sam. Their memories have made him conscious of the man's presence in his life.*] How old are you, Sam?

SAM: Two score and five.

365 HALLY: Strange, isn't it?

SAM: What?

HALLY: Me and you.

SAM: What's strange about it?

HALLY: Little white boy in short trousers and a black man old enough to be his father flying a kite. It's not every day you see that.

370 SAM: But why strange? Because the one is white and the other black?

HALLY: I don't know. Would have been just as strange, I suppose, if it had been me and my Dad . . . cripple man and a little boy! Nope! There's no chance of me flying a kite without it being strange. [*Simple statement of fact—no self-pity.*] There's a nice little short story there. "The Kite-Flyers." But we'd have to find a twist in the ending.

SAM: Twist?

HALLY: Yes. Something unexpected. The way it ended with us was too straightforward . . . me on the bench and you going back to work. There's no drama in that.

WILLIE: And me?

375 HALLY: You?

WILLIE: Yes me.

HALLY: You want to get into the story as well, do you? I got it! Change the title: "Afternoons in Sam's Room" . . . expand it and tell all the stories. It's on its way to being a novel. Our days in the old Jubilee. Sad in a way that they're over. I almost wish we were still in that little room.

SAM: We're still together.

HALLY: That's true. It's just that life felt the right size in there . . . not too big and not too small. Wasn't so hard to work up a bit of courage. It's got so bloody complicated since then.

The telephone rings. Sam answers it.

380 SAM: St. George's Park Tea Room . . . Hello, Madam . . . Yes, Madam, he's here . . . Hally, it's your mother.

HALLY: Where is she phoning from?

SAM: Sounds like the hospital. It's a public telephone.

HALLY: [*Relieved.*] You see! I told you. [*The telephone.*] Hello, Mom . . . Yes . . . Yes no fine. Everything's under control here. How's things with poor old Dad? . . . Has he had a bad turn? . . .

What? . . . Oh, God! . . . Yes, Sam told me, but I was sure he'd
made a mistake. But what's all this about, Mom? He didn't look
at all good last night. How can he get better so quickly? . . .
Then very obviously you must say no. Be firm with him. You're
the boss. . . . You know what it's going to be like if he comes
home. . . . Well, then, don't blame me when I fail my exams at
the end of the year. . . . Yes! How am I expected to be fresh for
school when I spend half the night massaging his gammy leg? . . .
So am I! . . . So tell him a white lie. Say Dr. Colley wants more
X-rays of his stump. Or bribe him. We'll sneak in double tots of
brandy in future. . . . What? . . . Order him to get back into bed
at once! If he's going to behave like a child, treat him like one. . . .
All right, Mom! I was just trying to . . . I'm sorry. . . . I said I'm
sorry. . . . Quick, give me your number. I'll phone you back. [*He
hangs up and waits a few seconds.*] Here we go again! [*He dials.*]
I'm sorry, Mom. . . . Okay . . . But now listen to me carefully. All
it needs is for you to put your foot down. Don't take no for an
answer. . . . Did you hear me? And whatever you do, don't discuss
it with him. . . . Because I'm frightened you'll give in to him. . . .
Yes, Sam gave me lunch. . . . I ate all of it! . . . No, Mom not a
soul. It's still raining here. . . . Right, I'll tell them. I'll just do
some homework and then lock up. . . . But remember now, Mom.
Don't listen to anything he says. And phone me back and let me
know what happens. . . . Okay. Bye, Mom. [*He hangs up. The men
are staring at him.*] My Mom says that when you're finished with
the floors you must do the windows. [*Pause.*] Don't misunderstand
me, chaps. All I want is for him to get better. And if he was, I'd
be the first person to say: "Bring him home." But he's not, and we
can't give him the medical care and attention he needs at home.
That's what hospitals are there for. [*Brusquely.*] So don't just
stand there! Get on with it!

Sam clears Hally's table.

You heard right. My Dad wants to go home.
SAM: Is he better?
385 HALLY: [*Sharply.*] No! How the hell can he be better when last night
he was groaning with pain? This is not an age of miracles!
SAM: Then he should stay in hospital.
HALLY: [*Seething with irritation and frustration.*] Tell me something I
don't know, Sam. What the hell do you think I was saying to my
Mom? All I can say is fuck-it-all.

SAM: I'm sure he'll listen to your Mom.

HALLY: You don't know what she's up against. He's already packed his shaving kit and pajamas and is sitting on his bed with his crutches, dressed and ready to go. I know him when he gets in that mood. If she tries to reason with him, we've had it. She's no match for him when it comes to a battle of words. He'll tie her up in knots. [*Trying to hid his true feelings.*]

390 SAM: I suppose it gets lonely for him in there.

HALLY: With all the patients and nurses around? Regular visits from the Salvation Army? Balls! It's ten times worse for him at home. I'm at school and my mother is here in the business all day.

SAM: He's at least got you at night.

HALLY: [*Before he can stop himself.*] And we've got him! Please! I don't want to talk about it anymore. [*Unpacks his school case, slamming down books on the table.*] Life is just a plain bloody mess, that's all. And people are fools.

SAM: Come on, Hally.

395 HALLY: Yes, they are! They bloody well deserve what they get.

SAM: Then don't complain.

HALLY: Don't try to be clever, Sam. It doesn't suit you. Anybody who thinks there's nothing wrong with this world needs to have his head examined. Just when things are going along all right, without fail someone or something will come along and spoil everything. Somebody should write that down as a fundamental law of the Universe. The principle of perpetual disappointment. If there is a God who created this world, he should scrap it and try again.

SAM: All right, Hally, all right. What you got for homework?

HALLY: Bullshit, as usual. [*Opens an exercise book and reads.*] "Write five hundred words describing an annual event of cultural or historical significance."

400 SAM: That should be easy enough for you.

HALLY: And also plain bloody boring. You know what he wants, don't you? One of their useless old ceremonies. The commemoration of the landing of the 1820 Settlers,[6] or if it's going to be culture, Carols by Candlelight every Christmas.

SAM: It's an impressive sight. Make a good description, Hally. All those candles glowing in the dark and the people singing hymns.

---

[6] In 1820 the British government paid for four thousand Britons to travel to the Cape and allotted each family one hundred acres.

HALLY: And it's called religious hysteria. [*Intense irritation.*] Please, Sam! Just leave me alone and let me get on with it. I'm not in the mood for games this afternoon. And remember my Mom's orders . . . you're to help Willie with the windows. Come on now, I don't want any more nonsense in here.

SAM: Okay, Hally, okay.

Hally settles down to his homework; determined preparations . . . pen, ruler, exercise book, dictionary, another cake . . . all of which will lead to nothing.

[*Sam waltzes over to Willie and starts to replace tables and chairs. He practices a ballroom step while doing so. Willie watches. When Sam is finished, Willie tries.*] Good! But just a little bit quicker on the turn and only move in to her after she's crossed over. What about this one?

Another step. When Sam is finished, Willie again has a go.

Much better. See what happens when you just relax and enjoy yourself? Remember that in two weeks' time and you'll be all right.

405   WILLIE: But I haven't got partner, Boet Sam.

SAM: Maybe Hilda will turn up tonight.

WILLIE: No, Boet Sam. [*Reluctantly.*] I gave her a good hiding.

SAM: You mean a bad one.

WILLIE: Good bad one.

410   SAM: Then you mustn't complain either. Now you pay the price for losing your temper.

WILLIE: I also pay two pounds ten shilling entrance fee.

SAM: They'll refund you if you withdraw now.

WILLIE: [*Appalled.*] You mean, don't dance?

SAM: Yes.

415   WILLIE: No! I wait too long and I practice too hard. If I find me new partner, you think I can be ready in two weeks? I ask Madam for my leave now and we practice every day.

SAM: Quickstep nonstop for two weeks. World record, Willie, but you'll be mad at the end.

WILLIE: No jokes, Boet Sam.

SAM: I'm not joking.

WILLIE: So then what?

420   SAM: Find Hilda. Say you're sorry and promise you won't beat her
               again.

      WILLIE: No.

      SAM: Then withdraw. Try again next year.

      WILLIE: No.

      SAM: Then I give up.

425   WILLIE: Haaikona, Boet Sam, you can't.

      SAM: What do you mean, I can't? I'm telling you: I give up.

      WILLIE: [*Adamant.*] No! [*Accusingly.*] It was you who start me ball-
               room dancing.

      SAM: So?

      WILLIE: Before that I use to be happy. And is you and Miriam who
               bring me to Hilda and say here's partner for you.

430   SAM: What are you saying, Willie?

      WILLIE: You!

      SAM: But me what? To blame?

      WILLIE: Yes.

      SAM: Willie . . . ? [*Bursts into laughter.*]

435   WILLIE: And now all you do is make jokes at me. You wait. When
               Miriam leaves you is my turn to laugh. Ha! Ha! Ha!

      SAM: [*He can't take Willie seriously any longer.*] She can leave me
               tonight! I know what to do. [*Bowing before an imaginary partner.*]
               May I have the pleasure? [*He dances and sings.*]
               "Just a fellow with his pillow . . .
               Dancin' like a willow . . .
               In an autumn breeze . . ."

      WILLIE: There you go again!

Sam goes on dancing and singing.

      Boet Sam!

      SAM: There's the answer to your problem! Judges' announcement in
               two weeks' time: "Ladies and gentlemen, the winner in the open
               section . . . Mr. Willie Malopo and his pillow!"

*This is too much for a now really angry Willie. He goes for Sam, but the latter is
too quick for him and puts Hally's table between the two of them.*

      HALLY: [*Exploding.*] For Christ's sake, you two!

440   WILLIE: [*Still trying to get at Sam.*] I donner you, Sam! Struesgod!

      SAM: [*Still laughing.*] Sorry, Willie . . . Sorry . . .

HALLY: Sam! Willie! [*Grabs his ruler and gives Willie a vicious whack on the bum.*] How the hell am I supposed to concentrate with the two of you behaving like bloody children!

WILLIE: Hit him too!

HALLY: Shut up, Willie.

445 WILLIE: He started jokes again.

HALLY: Get back to your work. You too, Sam. [*His ruler.*] Do you want another one, Willie?

Sam and Willie return to their work. Hally uses the opportunity to escape from his unsuccessful attempt at homework. He struts around like a little despot, ruler in hand, giving vent to his anger and frustration.

Suppose a customer had walked in then? Or the Park Superintendent. And seen the two of you behaving like a pair of hooligans. That would have been the end of my mother's license, you know. And your jobs! Well, this is the end of it. From now on there will be no more of your ballroom nonsense in here. This is a business establishment, not a bloody New Brighton dancing school. I've been far too lenient with the two of you. [*Behind the counter for a green cool drink and a dollop of ice cream. He keeps up his tirade as he prepares it.*] But what really makes me bitter is that I allow you chaps a little freedom in here when business is bad and what do you do with it? The foxtrot! Specially you, Sam. There's more to life than trotting around a dance floor and I thought at least you knew it.

SAM: It's a harmless pleasure, Hally. It doesn't hurt anybody.

HALLY: It's also a rather simple one, you know.

SAM: You reckon so? Have you ever tried?

450 HALLY: Of course not.

SAM: Why don't you? Now.

HALLY: What do you mean? Me dance?

SAM: Yes. I'll show you a simple step—the waltz—then you try it.

HALLY: What will that prove?

455 SAM: That it might not be as easy as you think.

HALLY: I didn't say it was easy. I said it was simple—like in simple-minded, meaning mentally retarded. You can't exactly say it challenges the intellect.

SAM: It does other things.

HALLY: Such as?

SAM: Make people happy.

460 HALLY: [*The glass in his hand.*] So do American cream sodas with ice cream. For God's sake, Sam, you're not asking me to take ball-room dancing serious, are you?

SAM: Yes.

HALLY: [*Sigh of defeat.*] Oh, well, so much for trying to give you a decent education. I've obviously achieved nothing.

SAM: You still haven't told me what's wrong with admiring something that's beautiful and then trying to do it yourself.

HALLY: Nothing. But we happen to be talking about a foxtrot, not a thing of beauty.

465 SAM: But that is just what I'm saying. If you were to see two champions doing, two masters of the art . . . !

HALLY: Oh, God, I give up. So now it's also art!

SAM: Ja.

HALLY: There's a limit, Sam. Don't confuse art and entertainment.

SAM: So then what is art?

470 HALLY: You want a definition?

SAM: Ja.

HALLY: [*He realizes he has got to be careful. He gives the matter a lot of thought before answering.*] Philosophers have been trying to do that for centuries. What is Art? What is Life? But basically I suppose it's . . . the giving of meaning to matter.

SAM: Nothing to do with beautiful?

HALLY: It goes beyond that. It's the giving of form to the formless.

475 SAM: Ja, well, maybe it's not art, then. But I still say it's beautiful.

HALLY: I'm sure the word you mean to use is entertaining.

SAM: [*Adamant.*] No. Beautiful. And if you want proof, come along to the Centenary Hall in New Brighton in two weeks' time.

The mention of the Centenary Hall draws Willie over to them.

HALLY: What for? I've seen the two of you prancing around in here often enough.

SAM: [*He laughs.*] This isn't the real thing, Hally. We're just playing around in here.

480 HALLY: So? I can use my imagination.

SAM: And what do you get?

HALLY: A lot of people dancing around and having a so-called good time.

SAM: That all?

HALLY: Well, basically it is that, surely.

485 SAM: No, it isn't. Your imagination hasn't helped you at all. There's a lot more to it than that. We're getting ready for the championships, Hally, not just another dance. There's going to be a lot of people, all right, and they're going to have a good time, but they'll only be spectators, sitting around and watching. It's just the competitors out there on the dance floor. Party decorations and fancy lights all around the walls! The ladies in beautiful evening dresses!

HALLY: My mother's got one of those, Sam, and quite frankly, it's an embarrassment every time she wears it.

SAM: [*Undeterred.*] Your imagination left out the excitement.

Hally scoffs.

Oh, yes. The finalists are not going to be out there just to have a good time. One of those couples will be the 1950 Eastern Province Champions. And your imagination left out the music.

WILLIE: Mr. Elijah Gladman Guzana and his Orchestral Jazzonions.

SAM: The sound of the big band, Hally. Trombone, trumpet, tenor and alto sax. And then, finally, your imagination also left out the climax of the evening when the dancing is finished, the judges have stopped whispering among themselves and the Master of Ceremonies collects their scorecards and goes up onto the stage to announce the winners.

490 HALLY: All right. So you make it sound like a bit of a do. It's an occasion. Satisfied?

SAM: [*Victory.*] So you admit that!

HALLY: Emotionally yes, intellectually no.

SAM: Well, I don't know what you mean by that, all I'm telling you is that it is going to be *the* event of the year in New Brighton. It's been sold out for two weeks already. There's only standing room left. We've got competitors coming from Kingwilliamstown, East London, Port Alfred.

Hally starts pacing thoughtfully.

HALLY: Tell me a bit more.

495 SAM: I thought you weren't interested . . . intellectually.

HALLY: [*Mysteriously.*] I've got my reasons.

SAM: What do you want to know?

HALLY: It takes place every year?

SAM: Yes. But only every third year in New Brighton. It's East London's turn to have the championships next year.

500 HALLY: Which, I suppose, makes it an even more significant event.

SAM: Ah ha! We're getting somewhere. Our "occasion" is now a "significant event."

HALLY: I wonder.

SAM: What?

HALLY: I wonder if I would get away with it.

505 SAM: But what?

HALLY: [*To the table and his exercise book.*] "Write five hundred words describing an annual event of cultural or historical significance." Would I be stretching poetic license a little too far if I called your ballroom championships a cultural event?

SAM: You mean . . . ?

HALLY: You think we could get five hundred words out of it, Sam?

SAM: Victor Sylvester has written a whole book on ballroom dancing.

510 WILLIE: You going to write about it, Master Hally?

HALLY: Yes, gentlemen, that is precisely what I am considering doing. Old Doc Bromely—he's my English teacher—is going to argue with me, of course. He doesn't like natives. But I'll point out to him that in strict anthropological terms the culture of a primitive black society includes its dancing and singing. To put my thesis in a nutshell: The war-dance has been replaced by the waltz. But it still amounts to the same thing: the release of primitive emotions through movement. Shall we give it a go?

SAM: I'm ready.

WILLIE: Me also.

HALLY: Ha! This will teach the old bugger a lesson. [*Decision taken.*] Right. Let's get ourselves organized. [*This means another cake on the table. He sits.*] I think you've given me enough general atmosphere, Sam, but to build the tension and suspense I need facts. [*Pencil poised.*]

515 WILLIE: Give him facts, Boet Sam.

HALLY: What you called the climax . . . how many finalists?

SAM: Six couples.

HALLY: [*Making notes.*] Go on. Give me the picture.

SAM: Spectators seated right around the hall. [*Willie becomes a spectator.*]

520 HALLY: . . . and it's a full house.

SAM: At one end, on the stage, Gladman and his Orchestral Jazzonions. At the other end is a long table with the three judges.
The six finalists go onto the dance floor and take up their positions. When they are ready and the spectators have settled down,
the Master of Ceremonies goes to the microphone. To start with,
he makes some jokes to get the people laughing . . .

HALLY: Good touch! [*As he writes.*] ". . . creating a relaxed atmosphere which will change to one of tension and drama as the climax is approached."

SAM: [*Onto a chair to act out the M.C.*] "Ladies and gentlemen, we
come now to the great moment you have all been waiting for this
evening. . . . The finals of the 1950 Eastern Province Open Ballroom Dancing Championships. But first let me introduce the
finalists! Mr. and Mrs. Welcome Tchabalala from Kingwilliamstown . . ."

WILLIE: [*He applauds after every name.*] Is when the people clap their
hands and whistle and make a lot of noise, Master Hally.

525   SAM: "Mr. Mulligan Njikelane and Miss Nomhle Nkonyeni of Gra-
hamstown; Mr. and Mrs. Norman Nchinga from Port Alfred;
Mr. Fats Bokolane and Miss Dina Plaatjies from East London;
Mr. Sipho Dugu and Mrs. Mable Magada from Peddie; and
from New Brighton our very own Mr. Willie Malopo and Miss
Hilda Samuels."

*Willie can't believe his ears. He abandons his role as spectator and scrambles into
position as a finalist.*

WILLIE: Relaxed and ready to romance!

SAM: The applause dies down. When everybody is silent, Gladman
lifts up his sax, nods at the Orchestral Jazzonions . . .

WILLIE: Play the jukebox please, Boet Sam!

SAM: I also only got bus fare, Willie.

530   HALLY: Hold it, everybody. [*Heads for the cash register behind the
counter.*] How much is in the till, Sam?

SAM: Three shillings. Hally . . . your Mom counted it before she left.

Hally hesitates.

HALLY: Sorry, Willie. You know how she carried on the last time I
did it. We'll just have to pool our combined imaginations and

hope for the best. [*Returns to the table.*] Back to work. How are
the points scored, Sam?

SAM: Maximum of ten points each for individual style, deportment,
rhythm and general appearance.

WILLIE: Must I start?

535 HALLY: Hold it for a second, Willie. And penalties?

SAM: For what?

HALLY: For doing something wrong. Say you stumble or bump into
somebody . . . do they take off any points?

SAM: [*Aghast.*] Hally . . . !

HALLY: When you're dancing. If you and your partner collide into
another couple.

*Hally can get no further. Sam has collapsed with laughter. He explains to
Willie.*

540 SAM: If me and Miriam bump into you and Hilda . . .

Willie joins him in another good laugh.

Hally, Hally . . . !

HALLY: [*Perplexed.*] Why? What did I say?

SAM: There's no collisions out there, Hally. Nobody trips or stumbles
or bumps into anybody else. That's what that moment is all
about. To be one of those finalists on that dance floor is like . . .
like being in a dream about a world in which accidents don't
happen.

HALLY: [*Genuinely moved by Sam's image.*] Jesus, Sam! That's beautiful!

WILLIE: [*Can endure waiting no longer.*] I'm starting! [*Willie dances
while Sam talks.*]

545 SAM: Of course it is. That's what I've been trying to say to you all
afternoon. And it's beautiful because that is what we want life to
be like. But instead, like you said, Hally, we're bumping into each
other all the time. Look at the three of us this afternoon: I've
bumped into Willie, the two of us have bumped into you, you've
bumped into your mother, she bumping into your Dad. . . . None
of us knows the steps and there's no music playing. And it doesn't
stop with us. The whole world is doing it all the time. Open a
newspaper and what do you read? America has bumped into Rus-
sia, England is bumping into India, rich man bumps into poor

man. Those are big collisions, Hally. They make for a lot of
bruises. People get hurt in all that bumping, and we're sick and
tired of it now. It's been going on for too long. Are we never going to get it right? . . . Learn to dance life like champions instead
of always being just a bunch of beginners at it?

HALLY: [*Deep and sincere admiration of the man.*] You've got a vision,
Sam!

SAM: Not just me. What I'm saying to you is that everybody's got it.
That's why there's only standing room left for the Centenary Hall
in two weeks' time. For as long as the music lasts, we are going to
see six couples get it right, the way we want life to be.

HALLY: But is that the best we can do, Sam . . . watch six finalists
dreaming about the way it should be?

SAM: I don't know. But it starts with that. Without the dream we
won't know what we're going for. And anyway I reckon there are
a few people who have got past just dreaming about it and are
trying for something real. Remember that thing we read once in
the paper about the Mahatma Gandhi? Going without food to
stop those riots in India?

550 HALLY: You're right. He certainly was trying to teach people to get
the steps right.

SAM: And the Pope.

HALLY: Yes, he's another one. Our old General Smuts as well, you
know. He's also out there dancing. You know, Sam, when you
come to think of it, that's what the United Nations boils down
to . . . a dancing school for politicians!

SAM: And let's hope they learn.

HALLY: [*A little surge of hope.*] You're right. We mustn't despair.
Maybe there's some hope for mankind after all. Keep it up,
Willie. [*Back to his table with determination.*] This is a lot bigger
than I thought. So what have we got? Yes, our title: "A World
Without Collisions."

555 SAM: That sounds good! "A World Without Collisions."

HALLY: Subtitle: "Global Politics on the Dance Floor." No. A bit too
heavy, hey? What about "Ballroom Dancing as a Political Vision"?

The telephone rings. Sam answers it.

SAM: St. George's Park Tea Room . . . Yes, Madam . . . Hally, it's
your Mom.

HALLY: [*Back to reality.*] Oh, God, yes! I'd forgotten all about that. Shit! Remember my words, Sam? Just when you're enjoying yourself, someone or something will come along and wreck everything.

SAM: You haven't heard what she's got to say yet.

560 HALLY: Public telephone?

SAM: No.

HALLY: Does she sound happy or unhappy?

SAM: I couldn't tell. [*Pause.*] She's waiting, Hally.

HALLY: [*To the telephone.*] Hello, Mom . . . No, everything is okay here. Just doing my homework. . . . What's your news? . . . You've what? . . . [*Pause. He takes the receiver away from his ear for a few seconds. In the course of Hally's telephone conversation, Sam and Willie discreetly position the stacked tables and chairs. Hally places the receiver back to his ear.*] Yes, I'm still here. Oh, well, I give up now. Why did you do it, Mom? . . . Well, I just hope you know what you've let us in for. . . . [*Loudly.*] I said I hope you know what you've let us in for! It's the end of the peace and quiet we've been having. [*Softly.*] Where is he? [*Normal voice.*] He can't hear us from in there. But for God's sake, Mom, what happened? I told you to be firm with him. . . . Then you and the nurses should have held him down, taken his crutches away. . . . I know only too well he's my father! . . . I'm not being disrespectful, but I'm sick and tired of emptying stinking chamberpots full of phlegm and piss. . . . Yes, I do! When you're not there, he asks *me* to do it. . . . If you really want to know the truth, that's why I've got no appetite for my food. . . . Yes! There's a lot of things you don't know about. For your information, I still haven't got that science textbook I need. And you know why? He borrowed the money you gave me for it. . . . Because I didn't want to start another fight between you two. . . . He says that every time. . . . All right, Mom! [*Viciously.*] Then just remember to start hiding your bag away again, because he'll be at your purse before long for money for booze. And when he's well enough to come down here, you better keep an eye on the till as well, because that is also going to develop a leak. . . . Then don't complain to me when he starts his old tricks. . . . Yes, you do. I get it from you on one side and from him on the other, and it makes life hell for me. I'm not going to be the peacemaker anymore. I'm warning you now: when the two of you start fighting again, I'm leaving home. . . . Mom, if you

start crying, I'm going to put down the receiver. . . . Okay . . .
[*Lowering his voice to a vicious whisper.*] Okay, Mom. I heard you.
[*Desperate.*] No. . . . Because I don't want to. I'll see him when I
get home! Mom! . . . [*Pause. When he speaks again, his tone changes
completely. It is not simply pretense. We sense a genuine emotional
conflict.*] Welcome home, chum! . . . What's that? . . . Don't be
silly, Dad. You being home is just about the best news in the
world. . . . I bet you are. Bloody depressing there with everybody
going on about their ailments, hey! . . . How you feeling? . . .
Good . . . Here as well, pal. Coming down cats and dogs. . . .
That's right. Just the day for a kip and a toss in your old Uncle
Ned. . . . Everything's just hunky-dory on my side, Dad. . . .
Well, to start with, there's a nice pile of comics for you on the
counter. . . . Yes, old Kemple brought them in. *Batman and
Robin, Submariner* . . . just your cup of tea . . . I will. . . . Yes, we'll
spin a few yarns tonight. . . . Okay, chum, see you in a little
while. . . . No, I promise, I'll come straight home. . . . [*Pause—his
mother comes back on the phone.*] Mom? Okay. I'll lock up now. . . .
What? . . . Oh, the brandy . . . Yes, I'll remember! . . . I'll put it in
my suitcase now, for God's sake. I know well enough what will
happen if he doesn't get it. . . . [*Places a bottle of brandy on the
counter.*] I *was* kind to him, Mom. I didn't say anything nasty! . . .
All right. Bye. [*End of telephone conversation. A desolate Hally
doesn't move. A strained silence.*]

565 SAM: [*Quietly.*] That sounded like a bad bump, Hally.

HALLY: [*Having a hard time controlling his emotions. He speaks carefully.*] Mind your own business, Sam.

SAM: Sorry. I wasn't trying to interfere. Shall we carry on? Hally?
[*He indicates the exercise book. No response from Hally.*]

WILLIE: [*Also trying.*] Tell him about when they give out the cups,
Boet Sam.

SAM: Ja! That's another big moment. The presentation of the cups
after the winners have been announced. You've got to put that in.

Still no response from Hally.

570 WILLIE: A big silver one, Master Hally, called floating trophy for the
champions.

SAM: We always invite some big-shot personality to hand them over.
Guest of honor this year is going to be His Holiness Bishop
Jabulani of the All African Free Zionist Church.

Hally gets up abruptly, goes to his table and tears up the page he was writing on.

HALLY: So much for a bloody world without collisions.

SAM: Too bad. It was on its way to being a good composition.

HALLY: Let's stop bullshitting ourselves, Sam.

575   SAM: Have we been doing that?

HALLY: Yes! That's what all our talk about a decent world has been . . . just so much bullshit.

SAM: We did say it was still only a dream.

HALLY: And a bloody useless one at that. Life's a fuck-up and it's never going to change.

SAM: Ja, maybe that's true.

580   HALLY: There's no maybe about it. It's a blunt and brutal fact. All we've done this afternoon is waste our time.

SAM: Not if we'd got your homework done.

HALLY: I don't give a shit about my homework, so, for Christ's sake, just shut up about it. [*Slamming books viciously into his school case.*] Hurry up now and finish your work. I want to lock up and get out of here. [*Pause.*] And then go where? Home-sweet-fucking-home. Jesus, I hate that word.

Hally goes to the counter to put the brandy bottle and comics in his school case. After a moment's hesitation, he smashes the bottle of brandy. He abandons all further attempts to hide his feelings. Sam and Willie work away as unobtrusively as possible.

Do you want to know what is really wrong with your lovely little dream, Sam? It's not just that we are all bad dancers. That does happen to be perfectly true, but there's more to it than just that. You left out the cripples.

SAM: Hally!

HALLY: [*Now totally reckless.*] Ja! Can't leave them out, Sam. That's why we always end up on our backsides on the dance floor. They're also out there dancing . . . like a bunch of broken spiders trying to do the quickstep! [*An ugly attempt at laughter.*] When you come to think of it, it's a bloody comical sight. I mean, it's bad enough on two legs . . . but one and a pair of crutches! Hell, no, Sam. That's guaranteed to turn that dance floor into a shambles. Why you shaking your head? Picture it, man. For once this afternoon let's use our imaginations sensibly.

585   SAM: Be careful, Hally.

HALLY: Of what? The truth? I seem to be the only one around here who is prepared to face it. We've had the pretty dream, it's time now to wake up and have a good long look at the way things really are. Nobody knows the steps, there's no music, the cripples are also out there tripping up everybody and trying to get into the act, and it's all called the All-Comers-How-to-Make-a-Fuckup-of-Life Championships. [*Another ugly laugh.*] Hang on, Sam! The best bit is still coming. Do you know what the winner's trophy is? A beautiful big chamber-pot with roses on the side, and it's full to the brim with piss. And guess who I think is going to be this year's winner.

SAM: [*Almost shouting.*] Stop now!

HALLY: [*Suddenly appalled by how far he has gone.*] Why?

SAM: Hally? It's your father you're talking about.

590 HALLY: So?

SAM: Do you know what you've been saying?

Hally can't answer. He is rigid with shame. Sam speaks to him sternly.

No, Hally, you mustn't do it. Take back those words and ask for forgiveness! It's a terrible sin for a son to mock his father with jokes like that. You'll be punished if you carry on. Your father is your father, even if he is a . . . cripple man.

WILLIE: Yes, Master Hally. Is true what Sam say.

SAM: I understand how you are feeling, Hally, but even so . . .

HALLY: No, you don't!

595 SAM: I think I do.

HALLY: And I'm telling you you don't. Nobody does. [*Speaking carefully as his shame turns to rage at Sam.*] It's your turn to be careful, Sam. Very careful! You're treading on dangerous ground. Leave me and my father alone.

SAM: I'm not the one who's been saying things about him.

HALLY: What goes on between me and my Dad is none of your business!

SAM: Then don't tell me about it. If that's all you've got to say about him, I don't want to hear.

For a moment Hally is at loss for a response.

600 HALLY: Just get on with your bloody work and shut up.

SAM: Swearing at me won't help you.

HALLY: Yes, it does! Mind your own fucking business and shut up!

SAM: Okay. If that's the way you want it, I'll stop trying.

He turns away. This infuriates Hally even more.

HALLY: Good. Because what you've been trying to do is meddle in something you know nothing about. All that concerns you here, Sam, is to try and do what you get paid for—keep the place clean and serve the customers. In plain words, just get on with your job. My mother is right. She's always warning me about allowing you to get too familiar. Well, this time you've gone too far. It's going to stop right now.

No response from Sam.

You're only a servant in here, and don't forget it.

Still no response. Hally is trying hard to get one.

And as far as my father is concerned, all you need to remember is that he is your boss.

605   SAM: [*Needled at last.*] No, he isn't. I get paid by your mother.

HALLY: Don't argue with me, Sam!

SAM: Then don't say he's my boss.

HALLY: He's a white man and that's good enough for you.

SAM: I'll try to forget you said that.

610   HALLY: Don't! Because you won't be doing me a favor if you do. I'm telling you to remember it.

A pause. Sam pulls himself together and makes one last effort.

SAM: Hally, Hally . . . ! Come on now. Let's stop before it's too late. You're right. We *are* on dangerous ground. If we're not careful, somebody is going to get hurt.

HALLY: It won't be me.

SAM: Don't be so sure.

HALLY: I don't know what you're talking about, Sam.

615   SAM: Yes, you do.

HALLY: [*Furious.*] Jesus, I wish you would stop trying to tell me what I do and what I don't know.

Sam gives up. He turns to Willie.

> SAM: Let's finish up.
>
> HALLY: Don't turn your back on me! I haven't finished talking.

He grabs Sam by the arm and tries to make him turn around. Sam reacts with a flash of anger.

> SAM: Don't do that, Hally! [*Facing the boy.*] All right, I'm listening. Well? What do you want to say to me?
>
> 620 HALLY: [*Pause as Hally looks for something to say.*] To begin with, why don't you also start calling me Master Harold, like Willie.
>
> SAM: Do you mean that?
>
> HALLY: Why the hell do you think I said it?
>
> SAM: And if I don't.
>
> HALLY: You might just lose your job.
>
> 625 SAM: [*Quietly and very carefully.*] If you make me say it once, I'll never call you anything else again.
>
> HALLY: So? [*The boy confronts the man.*] Is that meant to be a threat?
>
> SAM: Just telling you what will happen if you make me do that. You must decide what it means to you.
>
> HALLY: Well, I have. It's good news. Because that is exactly what Master Harold wants from now on. Think of it as a little lesson in respect, Sam, that's long overdue, and I hope you remember it as well as you do your geography. I can tell you now that somebody who will be glad to hear I've finally given it to you will be my Dad. Yes! He agrees with my Mom. He's always going on about it as well. "You must teach the boys to show you more respect, my son."
>
> SAM: So now you can stop complaining about going home. Everybody is going to be happy tonight.
>
> 630 HALLY: That's perfectly correct. You see, you mustn't get the wrong idea about me and my Dad, Sam. We also have our good times together. Some bloody good laughs. He's got a marvelous sense of humor. Want to know what our favorite joke is? He gives out a big groan, you see, and says: "It's not fair, is it, Hally?" Then I have to ask: "What, chum?" And then he says: "A nigger's arse" . . . and we both have a good laugh.

The men stare at him with disbelief.

What's the matter, Willie? Don't you catch the joke? You always were a bit slow on the uptake. It's what is called a pun. You see, fair means both light in color and to be just and decent. [*He turns to Sam.*] I thought *you* would catch it, Sam.

SAM: Oh ja, I catch it all right.

HALLY: But it doesn't appeal to your sense of humor.

SAM: Do you really laugh?

HALLY: Of course.

635 SAM: To please him? Make him feel good?

HALLY: No, for heaven's sake! I laugh because I think it's a bloody good joke.

SAM: You're really trying hard to be ugly, aren't you? And why drag poor old Willie into it? He's done nothing to you except show you the respect you want so badly. That's also not being fair, you know . . . and *I* mean just or decent.

WILLIE: It's all right, Sam. Leave it now.

SAM: It's me you're after. You should just have said "Sam's arse" . . . because that's the one you're trying to kick. Anyway, how do you know it's not fair? You've never seen it. Do you want to? [*He drops his trousers and underpants and presents his backside for Hally's inspection.*] Have a good look. A real Basuto[7] arse . . . which is about as nigger as they can come. Satisfied? [*Trousers up.*] Now you can make your Dad even happier when you go home tonight. Tell him I showed you my arse and he is quite right. It's not fair. And if it will give him an even better laugh next time, I'll also let *him* have a look. Come, Willie, let's finish up and go.

Sam and Willie start to tidy up the tea room. Hally doesn't move. He waits for a moment when Sam passes him.

640 HALLY: [*Quietly.*] Sam . . .

Sam stops and looks expectantly at the boy. Hally spits in his face. A long and heartfelt groan from Willie. For a few seconds Sam doesn't move.

SAM: [*Taking out a handkerchief and wiping his face.*] It's all right, Willie.

---

7 any of a Bantu people living in Basutoland, or Lesotho, in southeast Africa

To Hally.

> Ja, well, you've done it . . . Master Harold. Yes, I'll start calling
> you that from now on. It won't be difficult anymore. You've hurt
> yourself, Master Harold. I saw it coming. I warned you, but you
> wouldn't listen. You've just hurt yourself *bad.* And you're a cow-
> ard, Master Harold. The face you should be spitting in is your
> father's . . . but you used mine, because you think you're safe in-
> side your fair skin . . . and this time I don't mean just or decent.
> [*Pause, then moving violently towards Hally.*] Should I hit him,
> Willie?

WILLIE: [*Stopping Sam.*] No, Boet Sam.

SAM: [*Violently.*] Why not?

WILLIE: It won't help, Boet Sam.

645 SAM: I don't want to help! I want to hurt him.

WILLIE: You also hurt yourself.

SAM: And if he had done it to you, Willie?

WILLIE: Me? Spit at me like I was a dog? [*A thought that had not occurred to him before. He looks at Hally.*] Ja. Then I want to hit him.
I want to hit him hard!

*A dangerous few seconds as the men stand staring at the boy. Willie turns away,
shaking his head.*

> But maybe all I do is go cry at the back. He's little boy, Boet Sam.
> Little *white* boy. Long trousers now, but he's still little boy.

SAM: [*His violence ebbing away into defeat as quickly as it flooded.*]
You're right. So go on, then: groan again, Willie. You do it better
than me. [*To Hally.*] You don't know all of what you've just
done . . . Master Harold. It's not just that you've made me feel
dirtier than I've ever been in my life . . . I mean, how do I wash
off yours and your father's filth? . . . I've also failed. A long time
ago I promised myself I was going to try to do something, but
you've just shown me . . . Master Harold . . . that I've failed.
[*Pause.*] I've also got a memory of a little white boy when he was
still wearing short trousers and a black man, but they're not flying
a kite. It was the old Jubilee days, after dinner one night. I was in
my room. You came in and just stood against the wall, looking
down at the ground, and only after I'd asked you what you
wanted, what was wrong, I don't know how many times, did you
speak and even then so softly I almost didn't hear you. "Sam,

please help me to go and fetch my Dad." Remember? He was dead drunk on the floor of the Central Hotel Bar. They'd phoned for your Mom, but you were the only one at home. And do you remember how we did it? You went in first by yourself to ask permission for me to go into the bar. Then I loaded him onto my back like a baby and carried him back to the boarding house with you following behind carrying his crutches. [*Shaking his head as he remembers.*] A crowded Main Street with all the people watching a little white boy following his drunk father on a nigger's back! I felt for that little boy . . . Master Harold. I felt for him. After that we still had to clean him up, remember? He'd messed in his trousers, so we had to clean him up and get him into bed.

650   HALLY: [*Great pain.*] I love him, Sam.

SAM: I know you do. That's why I tried to stop you from saying these things about him. It would have been so simple if you could have just despised him for being a weak man. But he's your father. You love him and you're ashamed of him. You're ashamed of so much! . . . And now that's going to include yourself. That was the promise I made to myself: to try and stop that happening. [*Pause.*] After we got him to bed you came back with me to my room and sat in a corner and carried on just looking down at the ground. And for days after that! You hadn't done anything wrong, but you went around as if you owed the world an apology for being alive. I didn't like seeing that! That's not the way a boy grows up to be a man! . . . But the one person who should have been teaching you what that means was the cause of your shame. If you really want to know, that's why I made you that kite. I wanted you to look up, be proud of something, of yourself . . . [*Bitter smile at the memory.*] . . . and you certainly were that when I left you with it up there on the hill. Oh, ja . . . something else! . . . If you ever do write it as a short story, there *was* a twist in our ending. I couldn't sit down there and stay with you. It was a "Whites Only" bench. You were too young, too excited to notice then. But not anymore. If you're not careful . . . Master Harold . . . you're going to be sitting up there by yourself for a long time to come, and there won't be a kite in the sky. [*Sam has got nothing more to say. He exits into the kitchen, taking off his waiter's jacket.*]

WILLIE: Is bad. Is all all bad in here now.

HALLY: [*Books into his school case, raincoat on.*] Willie . . . [*It is difficult to speak.*] Will you lock up for me and look after the keys?

WILLIE: Okay.

Sam returns. Hally goes behind the counter and collects the few coins in the cash register. As he starts to leave . . .

655 SAM: Don't forget the comic books.

Hally returns to the counter and puts them in his case. He starts to leave again.

[*To the retreating back of the boy.*] Stop . . . Hally . . .

Hally stops, but doesn't turn to face him.

Hally . . . I've got no right to tell you what being a man means if I don't behave like one myself, and I'm not doing so well at that this afternoon. Should we try again, Hally?
HALLY: Try what?
SAM: Fly another kite, I suppose. It worked once, and this time I need it as much as you do.
HALLY: It's still raining, Sam. You can't fly kites on rainy days, remember.
SAM: So what do we do? Hope for better weather tomorrow?
660 HALLY: [*Helpless gesture.*] I don't know. I don't know anything anymore.
SAM: You sure of that, Hally? Because it would be pretty hopeless if that was true. It would mean nothing has been learnt in here this afternoon, and there was a hell of a lot of teaching going on . . . one way or the other. But anyway, I don't believe you. I reckon there's one thing you know. You don't *have* to sit up there by yourself. You know what that bench means now, and you can leave it any time you choose. All you've got to do is stand up and walk away from it.

Hally leaves. Willie goes up quietly to Sam.

WILLIE: Is okay, Boet Sam. You see. Is . . . [*He can't find any better words.*] . . . *is* going to be okay tomorrow. [*Changing his tone.*] Hey, Boet Sam! [*He is trying hard.*] You right. I think about it and you right. Tonight I find Hilda and say sorry. And make promise I won't beat her no more. You hear me, Boet Sam?
SAM: I hear you, Willie.
WILLIE: And when we practice I relax and romance with her from

beginning to end. Non-stop! You watch! Two weeks' time: "First prize for promising newcomers: Mr. Willie Malopo and Miss Hilda Samuels." [*Sudden impulse.*] To hell with it! I walk home. [*He goes to the jukebox, puts in a coin and selects a record. The machine comes to life in the gray twilight, blushing its way through a spectrum of soft, romantic colors.*] How did you say it, Boet Sam? Let's dream. [*Willie sways with the music and gestures for Sam to dance.*]

Sarah Vaughan sings.

> "Little man you're crying,
> I know why you're blue,
> Someone took your kiddy car away;
> Better go to sleep now,
> Little man you've had a busy day." [*etc. etc.*]
> You lead. I follow.

The men dance together.

> "Johnny won your marbles,
> Tell you what we'll do;
> Dad will get you new ones
>   right away;
> Better go to sleep now,
> Little man you've had a
>   busy day."

Discussion Questions

1. How is Hally's character shaped by his father's inadequacies? In what sense is he his father's son? In what sense does he try to compensate for his father's shortcomings?

2. In what ways is the relationship between Hally and Sam like and unlike a father-son relationship?

3. The play uses a personal relationship to make a statement about a social and political situation. In what respect can it be seen as also using political tensions to make a point about personal relationships?

4. Is the background of apartheid and South African social and cultural mores essential to the play, or could you imagine other settings and contexts in which Sam might be vulnerable to Hally's mistreatment? Do you think the play is dated now that apartheid has been abolished?

5. Is Sam's failure to react with violence realistic? What other options are available to him?

6. What is Willie's function in the play? Does his presence affect the dynamics between Hally and Sam? Does it give the audience any essential information about the other two characters? How would the play be different without him?

7. What are the advantages and disadvantages of the play's focusing on only three characters and using a single setting? What could Fugard have gained by showing Hally, Sam, and Willie in other contexts? By having them interact with other characters?

8. Is the play's ending hopeful? Pessimistic? Cynical?

9. Hally seems obsessed with past events. What comment do you think Fugard is making through Hally about the past and its impact on the present?

10. What do Sam and Hally learn during the course of the play? How do you think this knowledge might affect their future lives?

Research Questions

1. Many critics have observed that Athol Fugard's plays are political in nature. Using biographical profiles and interviews listed in the bibliography of this book, determine whether or not Fugard's plays are primarily political works. How does Fugard himself characterize his plays? Does he suggest any political solutions for the racial situation in South Africa? Does he contend his plays are inspired by specific events or simply by the political climate of their settings? Do you think that Fugard's assessment of his motivation is accurate?

2. *"Master Harold"* . . . *and the boys* was first performed in 1982 at the Yale Repertory Theatre. How was this play received by the critics? How were subsequent performances received? Use the Internet to find some of your information.

3. Watch the videotaped recording of *"Master Harold"* . . . *and the boys* and compare it to the published play. Does the film version reflect the stage directions, dialogue, and sequence of events set forth in the written version of the play? Are there any elements in the film that differ from those in the written play? What would you say are the advantages and disadvantages of watching the filmed version of the play?

4. In Alisa Solomon's "'Look At History': An Interview with Zakes Mokae," on pages 88–95, Mokae offers some first-hand observations about Athol Fugard's career as a writer. Locate additional interviews with actors or directors of Fugard's plays as well as interviews or biographical profiles of Fugard himself. What can you infer from these sources about Fugard's concerns about South African society and about his writing? Are Fugard's concerns the same as those of Mokae and the others? In what ways are they different?

5. *"Master Harold"* . . . *and the boys* takes place in 1950, the year in which many laws were passed in South Africa to ensure racial segregation. Compare the state of race relations in South Africa during the 1950s with conditions in the United States at the same time. Consider specific laws that applied to African-Americans in the United States as well as policies of segregation in schools, the military, and so on. Do you believe that race relations in the United States were better than those in South Africa? Compare the legal positions of South African blacks and African-Americans during the 1950s.

6. Read a work by another South African writer—Nadine Gordimer, for example. Compare this work with *"Master Harold"* . . . *and the boys*. Do Fugard and the other writer treat similar themes? Do they portray both black and white characters? Do both writers see the same strengths and weaknesses in South African society?

Secondary Sources

Each of the eight sources in this section* offers insights into *"Master Harold"... and the boys*—insights that can help you understand, enjoy, and perhaps write about the play. The sources included in this section range from Fugard's autobiographical notes concerning the incident that suggested the play to critical articles commenting on specific ideas and scenes. You may choose to use these sources to generate ideas that could be developed into a paper; you may also find material that supports a paper topic that you have already chosen. Once you have read these sources, you can use the bibliography at the back of this book to locate further resources pertaining to Fugard's life and works as well as information about South Africa. Remember to document any words or ideas that you borrow from these and any other sources.

ERROL DURBACH

"Master Harold"... and the boys: Athol Fugard and the Psychopathology of Apartheid

In this play, dredged out of Athol Fugard's painful memories of a South African adolescence, at least one event stands out in joyous recollection: the boy's exhilarating, liberating, and ultimately transcendent experience of flying a kite made out of tomato-box slats, brown paper, discarded stockings, and string. From the scraps and leavings of the depressingly mundane, the boy intuits the meaning of a soul-life; and he responds to the experience

---

* Note that the Durbach, Vandenbroucke, Mshengu, and Jordan articles do not use the parenthetical documentation style recommended by the Modern Language Association and explained in the Appendix (pages 159–172).

as a "miracle."[1] "Why did you make that kite, Sam?" he asks of the black servant whose gift it was—but the answer is not given until much later in the play. Nor can Hally recollect the reason for Sam's failure to share in the experience of high-flying delight:

> HALLY: . . . You left me after that, didn't you? You explained how to get it down, we tied it to the bench so that I could sit and watch it, and you went away. I wanted you to stay, you know. I was a little scared of having to look after it by myself.
>
> SAM: [*Quietly.*] I had work to do, Hally.

In the final moments of the play Sam provides the simple explanation: the kite had been a symbolic gift to console the child against the degrading shame of having to cope with a drunken and crippled father—an attempt to raise his eyes from the ground of humiliation:

> That's not the way a boy grows up to be a man! . . . But the one person who should have been teaching you what that means was the cause of your shame. If you really want to know, that's why I made you that kite. I wanted you to look up, be proud of something, of yourself . . .

The second question has an answer more readily understood by one familiar with apartheid's so-called "petty" operations:

> I couldn't sit down there and stay with you. It was a "Whites Only" bench. You were too young, too excited to notice then. But not anymore. If you're not careful . . . Master Harold . . . you're going to be sitting up there by yourself for a long time to come, and there won't be a kite in the sky.

This, in essence, is the psychopathology of apartheid. Growing up to be a "man" within a system that deliberately sets out to humiliate black people, even to the point of relegating them to separate benches, entails the danger of habitual indifference to the everyday details that shape black/white relationships and, finally, pervert them. It is not merely that racial prejudice is *legislated* in South Africa. It insinuates itself into every social sphere of existence, until the very language of ordinary human discourse begins to reflect the policy that makes black men subservient to the power exercised by white children. Hally, the seventeen-year-old white boy whose affectionately diminutive name is an index of his social immaturity, is "Master Harold" in the context of attitudes fostered by apartheid. And the black man who is his mentor and surrogate father is the "boy"—in all but compassion, humanity, and moral intelligence.

This, finally, is the only definition that the South African system can conceive of in the relationship of White to Black; and Hally, with the facility of one habituated to such power play, saves face and forestalls criticism by rapidly realigning the components of friendship into the socio-political patterns of mastery and servitude. Like quicksilver, he shifts from intimate familiarity with his black companions, to patronizing condescension to his social inferiors, to an appalling exercise of power over the powerless "boys" simply by choosing to play the role of "baas":

> Sam! Willie! [*Grabs his ruler and gives Willie a vicious whack on the bum.*] How the hell am I supposed to concentrate with the two of you behaving like bloody children! [. . .] Get back to your work. You too, Sam. [*His ruler.*] Do you want another one, Willie?
> [*Sam and Willie return to their work. Hally uses the opportunity to escape from his unsuccessful attempt at homework. He struts around like a little despot, ruler in hand, giving vent to his anger and frustration.*]

Within the culture portrayed in the play there is nothing particularly remarkable about a white child hitting a black man. It would have been unheard of on the other hand for a black man, in the South Africa of the 1950s, to strike back. *His* anger and frustration could be unleashed only upon those even more pitifully dispossessed of the human rights to dignity and respect. The white child hits the black man, and the black man hits the black woman. It is a system in which violence spirals downwards in a hierarchy of degradation—as Fugard shows in Willie's relationship with his battered dancing partner who can no longer tolerate the abuse.

A very simple racial equation operates within apartheid: White = "Master"; Black = "Boy." It is an equation which ignores traditional relationships of labor to management, of paid employee to paying employer, or contractual relationships between freely consenting parties. And Sam's attempt to define the nature of his employment in conventional terms is countermanded by Hally's application of the equation:

> HALLY: You're only a servant here, and don't forget it. [. . .] And as far as
>   my father is concerned, all you need to remember is that he's your boss.
> SAM: [*Needled at last.*] No, he isn't. I get paid by your mother.
> HALLY: Don't argue with me, Sam!
> SAM: Then don't say he's my boss.
> HALLY: He's a white man and that's good enough for you.

What needles Sam is the thought of being paid for his work by a bigot who shows him none of the simple human respect that is everyone's most urgent *need* in Fugard's world—the white child's in a family that shames him, and the black man's in a culture that humiliates him. It is the common denominator that Sam and Hally share; and the ultimate goal of "Master" Harold's power-play is to secure his own desire for self-respect at the expense of a man whose native dignity proves all but impervious to these attempts to "boy" him. It is a self-defeating and self-destructive ploy, imposed by threat and blackmail upon a relationship which has all the potential for mutual comfort, support, and love. It is the human content of their shared affection that Hally is about to petrify into the equation of apartheid:

> HALLY: To begin with, why don't you also start calling me Master Harold, like Willie.
> SAM: [. . .] And if I don't?
> HALLY: You might lose your job.
> SAM: [*Quietly and very carefully.*] If you make me say it once, I'll never call you anything else again. [. . .] You must decide what it means to you.
> HALLY: Well, I have. It's good news. Because that is exactly what Master Harold wants from now on. Think of it as a little lesson in respect, Sam, that's long overdue. [. . .] I can tell you now that somebody who will be glad to hear I've finally given it to you will be my Dad. Yes! He agrees with my Mom. He's always going on about it as well. "You must teach the boys to show you more respect, my son."

"Teaching respect" loses all semantic value in the context of apartheid. It means coercion by threat, just as "showing respect" means acquiescence through enforced abasement. It is easy to teach Willie respect—one does it with the stick, and with impunity because Willie lacks the necessary sentiment of self-regard to oppose such treatment. His predictable response is to insist that Hally whack Sam as well—the sole comfort of the wretched being to recognize fellow-sufferers in distress. But Hally cannot *command* Sam's respect; and if he cannot *win* it, his only recourse is to humiliate Sam to the point where, by default, his own pathetic superiority supervenes. Finally, the only power left to Hally is the wounding power of bigotry supported by a system in which "black" is, *ipso facto*, base. Echoing his father's words, associating himself with the very cause of his shame, he spreads the "filth" he has been taught in a racist joke—the penultimate weapon in his arsenal of power. It is a crude pun about a "nigger's arse" not being "fair"; and one senses, in the numb incredulity of the two black men, an irreversible redefinition of their relationship with their white charge. In the ensuing silence, he belabors the pun—the double meaning of "fair" as light in color *and* just and decent—and is ensnared in the moral implications of his bid for respect through insult and abuse:

> SAM: You're really trying hard to be ugly, aren't you? And why drag poor Willie into it? He's done nothing to you except show you the respect you want so badly. That's also not being fair, you know . . . and *I* mean just or decent.

And to underscore the embarrassment that Hally has brought upon himself, Sam performs an action of rebuke through self-abasement that reveals both the reality and the vulnerability of the "nigger's arse"—the thing that the Master feels at liberty to mock at and kick: *"He drops his trousers and underpants and presents his backside for Hally's inspection."* His nakedness is clearly no laughing matter. It calls in question the justice and decency and fairness of an entire system which can encourage a child so to humiliate a man. Its indictment is Dostoievskian in its power to shame.

Hally's countermeasure is to exercise his power to degrade with impunity: he spits in Sam's face, saving his own by fouling another's and, in so doing, placing Sam forever in the role of "boy" to his "Master." It is a gesture of contempt and angry frustration, the adolescent's protest against his own sense of degradation—horribly misdirected against the wrong source, as Sam instantly realizes: "The face you should be spitting in," he says, "is your father's . . . but you used mine, because you think you're safe inside your fair skin . . . and this time I don't mean just or decent." It is Hally's "white" father who ensures the "principle of perpetual disappointment" in the boy's life—the crippled alcoholic who must be dragged out of bars fouled in his own excrement, whose chamber pots must be emptied by the boy, and whose imminent return from the hospital provokes in Hally the thought of further humiliating servitude. But it is Hally's black "father" who must bear the brunt of his anguish and his shame. Sam has become his "spitting boy" just as Willie has been his "whipping boy," the recipient of a contempt which he cannot reveal to his father, whom he both loves and despises. This is the moment, Fugard admitted in an interview, "which totally symbolized the ugliness, the potential ugliness waiting for me as a White South African."[2]

The overwhelming shame of the actual event is recorded in the section of Fugard's *Notebooks*[3] dealing with his childhood memories of growing up in Port Elizabeth. But he sets the play five years later, in 1950,[4] that *annus mirabilis* of Apartheid legislation; and Fugard's political point of view is nowhere more clearly revealed than in his location of the encroaching ugliness of South Africa's destiny in a *personal* rather than a *national* failure of moral decency. Despite the statutory enforcement of racist laws in the 1950s, apartheid (like charity) is seen to begin *at home*, in the small details of everyday existence. There is no sense, in the play, of the Nationalist Government's Population Registration Act of 1950 with its racial system of classification by color, the Group Areas Act of 1950 which demarcated the areas of permissible domicile for the races and controlled the ownership of property in those areas, the 1950 Amendment to the Immorality Act which prohibited sexual contact across the color bar, or the Suppression of Communism Act of 1950 which empowered the minister of Justice to ban suspect individuals without trial or right of appeal—indeed, without even notifying the detainee of the nature of his offense. There is nothing of Kafka's nightmare about Fugard's world, nothing of the political absurdity of Václav Havel's vision of man's soul under totalitarianism. Nor does he invoke the ridiculous terms of the Separate Amenities Act which, in 1953, would subject a black man sitting on a "Whites Only" bench ("reserved for the exclusive use of persons belonging to a particular race or class, being a race or class to which he does not belong")[5] to a fine not exceeding fifty pounds or imprisonment not exceeding three months, or to both.

Fugard's is not a drama of political protest nor an exposé of a corrupt regime entrenched in its position of power. His detractors on the militant Left call him bitterly to task for failing to fight against the system, just as his Right-wing detractors point to the obsolescence of his political vision—to the disappearance of "Whites Only" signs on South African benches in the 1980s. Plays like *Statements after an Arrest under the Immorality Act* or *Sizwe Bansi Is Dead* may, indeed, seem anachronistic after the rescinding of the Immorality Act and the Pass laws with which they deal. But the psychopathology of apartheid in Fugard's drama is quite distinct from Government policy. There is no guarantee, when the letter of all the 1950's legislation has passed into oblivion, that the *attitudes* which informed its spirit will disappear as well. The Laws are crucial historical background to Fugard's world, but these attitudes are the substance of his most insistent misgivings about apartheid's operation upon human relationships.

In the absence of explicit political comment, it might seem tendentious to equate the social awkwardness of a troubled teenager with government policy. Hally's condescending attitude towards his "boys," his failure to share with them any of the chocolate and cake and ice-cream that he is constantly consuming—these may be evidence of an ingrained arrogance and selfishness rather than a culturally conditioned attitude to an "inferior" race.

But these unobtrusive details underscore the more overt acts of insulting racism in the play. Having whacked one "boy" with a ruler and spat in the other's face, his last shamefaced act is to remove the wretched day's takings from the cash register—essentially small change—and tell Willie to lock up for him. One entrusts the "boy" with the keys to the tearoom, but not with the few coins which might tempt him to play the jukebox or take the bus home. One may *give* a "boy" some cake or chocolate, but never *offer* it. Every social gesture, within the South African context, becomes an affirmation or a negation of the principle of apartheid; and every act is more or less political.

Against the petty and unconscious cruelties of Hally, Fugard juxtaposes the magnanimity of Sam: the compassionate father, the good friend, the moral teacher. He offers a solution to the predicament, again in *personal* rather than *political* terms—a response so lacking in revolutionary fervor as to alienate, once again, the new generation of post-Sowetan critics of Athol Fugard's drama.[6] Mastering his violence and the desire to strike Hally for spitting at him, Sam carefully considers the strategy of aggression with Willie, and they both agree to suffer the indignity in stoical resignation:

> WILLIE: [. . .] But maybe all I do is go cry at the back. He's little boy, Boet Sam. Little *white* boy. Long trousers now, but he's still little boy.
> SAM: [*His violence ebbing away into defeat as quickly as it flooded.*] You're right. So go on, then: groan again, Willie. You do it better than me.

Though struck to the quick, they endure the insult with weeping and groaning rather than striking back. There is no revolution in the St. George's Park Tearoom—but not because the black man is culturally conditioned to patience, nor for fear of putting his job in jeopardy. In Fugard's world, as in Prospero's, the rarer action is in virtue than in vengeance, in humane reasoning rather than fury; and Sam trusts, once again, to his capacity for moving Master Harold to shame through moral suasion and exemplary behavior. He forgives the little white boy who knows no better, and behaves like a "man" in order to teach him the rudiments of "manly" behavior. Turning the other cheek may not be politically expedient as a response to apartheid, but where problems are engendered at the personal level it is only at the personal level that they may be resolved.

"I oscillate," says the precocious Hally early in the play, "between hope and despair for this world. . . . But things will change, you wait and see." On the whole, Sam's politics are ranged on the side of hope—the hope born, initially, of a naive vision of reform and racial harmony but modulating, in the final scenes, to the more somber hope of salvaging the scrap of value remaining in his relationship with the little white master. He dreams of a world transformed by some benevolent reformer—a savior like Napoleon for whom all men were equal before the law, or another Abraham Lincoln who fought for the oppressed, or a Tolstoy, or Gandhi, or Christ; and he envisions life as a celestial ballroom in which no accidents occur, in which powers are harmoniously aligned on the global dance floor. But, like Hally, he is forced to acknowledge the harsh reality of things: we go on waiting for the "Man of Magnitude," he admits, bumping and colliding until we're sick and tired. All that remains is the small gesture, the little act of decency that may turn a fragment of the dream into something real. This, finally, is what he hopes for. He takes off his servant's jacket and returns in clothes that no longer distinguish him as a "boy"; he addresses Hally by the affectionate diminutive once again; and he offers, very simply, the chance to "fly another kite." "You can't fly kites on rainy days," says Hally—and the rain and the wind squalling beyond the windows of the tearoom assume the depressing and hopeless condition of the entire South African situation. Better weather tomorrow? No one is sure.

At this point in the Yale Repertory production of the play,[7] the excellent Zakes Mokae playing Sam extends his hand tentatively towards Hally in a gesture of appeal and reconciliation as important to his well-being as to the boy's; and he challenges him to change the situation through an act of personal transformation which flies in the face of his cultural and political conditioning: "You don't *have* to sit up there by yourself," he says, recalling the boy's isolation on the "Whites Only" bench. You know what that bench means now, and you can leave it any time you choose. All you've got to do is stand up and walk away from it." But ingrained attitudes die hard. Paralyzed by shame but incapable of extending himself towards the black man, Hally hesitates and then walks out into the rains as Sam's hand crumples in its gesture.

If anyone has learned a lesson from this bleak afternoon of moral instruction it is the simple, inarticulate Willie who, in his effort to comfort Sam, endorses his dream-ideal of life as a ballroom. He vows never to beat up his partner again, and slips his bus fare into the jukebox which *"comes to life in the gray twilight, blushing its way through a spectrum of soft, romantic colors."* "Let's dream," he says. And the two men sway through the room to Sarah Vaughan's melancholy lullaby to an unhappy child—"Little man you're crying." The final dramatic image is suffused with the ambiguous tonalities typical of Fugard's best work: the rain of despair beyond the windows, the wind in which no kites fly, the hopelessness of a situation where people are driven apart by racist attitudes, the consoling music which evokes our compassion for children who are casualties of their upbringing, the hope that shame and embarrassment might induce change in a morally receptive child, the delusory political vision of racial harmony on the South African dance floor, and the image of a world where "Whites Only" leave two black men dancing together in an act of solidarity. It is a typically Fugardian oscillation between hope and despair, qualified only by the realization that "Master Harold" grows up to be Athol Fugard and that the play itself is an act of atonement and moral reparation to the memory of Sam and "H.D.F."—the Black and the White fathers to whom it is dedicated.

It would clearly be misleading to claim that *"Master Harold" . . . and the boys* addresses the growing complexity of apartheid politics in the South Africa of 1987. It is a "history" play—a *family* "history" written, like O'Neill's *Long Day's Journey into Night,* as an exorcism of the tormented ghosts of his childhood;[8] but it is also a phase of South African "history," an anachronistic backward glance to a time when black men in the stoical optimism still dreamed of social change and when white boys might have been able to grasp the implications of "Whites Only" benches and choose to walk away from them. It deals with a rite of passage clumsily negotiated, a failure of love in a personal power-struggle with political implications. Alan Paton, writing in the same time-frame of history, projects a similar vision of tenuous hope for racial harmony—and also the dreadful consequences of its deferment. Msimangu, the black priest in *Cry, the Beloved Country,* speaks the powerful subtext beneath the action of Fugard's play:

> But there is only one thing that has power completely, and that is love. Because when a man loves, he seeks no power, and therefore he has power. I see only one hope for our country, and that is when white men and black men, desiring neither power nor money, but desiring only the good of their country, come together to work for it.
>
> He was grave and silent, and then he said somberly, I have one great fear in my heart, that one day when they are turned to loving, they will find we are turned to hating.[9]

NOTES

[1] Athol Fugard, *"Master Harold" . . . and the boys* (New York, 1982). All quotations derive from this edition.

[2] Quoted in Dennis Walder, *Athol Fugard* (London, 1984), p. 120.

[3] Athol Fugard, *Notebooks: 1960–1977* (Johannesburg, 1983), pp. 25–26.

[4] Fugard (b. 1932) puts his age at thirteen in the *Notebooks,* but makes Hally a youth of seventeen.

⁵ "The Separate Amenities Act, No. 49 of 1953," in Edgar H. Brookes, *Apartheid: A Documentary Study of Modern South Africa* (London, 1968), p. 88.

⁶ I have discussed the general attitude of the African Marxists and the Black militant critics towards Fugard in "Sophocles in South Africa: Athol Fugard's *The Island,*" *Comparative Drama,* 18 (1984), pp. 252–264. The New York critic of *"Master Harold"* for the black paper, *Amsterdam News,* expressed disgust at a white writer who "set up a situation in which a black man's dignity is so assaulted by a little boy that he had the impulse to hit him . . . and didn't." Quoted by Margarete Seidenspinner, *Exploring the Labyrinth: Athol Fugard's Approach to South African Drama* (Essen, 1986), p. 211.

⁷ This version of the play, with Matthew Broderick as Hally, has been broadcast on PBS Television.

⁸ "I was dealing with the last unlaid ghost in my life, who was my father." Fugard, in Russell Vandenbroucke, *Truths the Hand Can Touch: The Theatre of Athol Fugard* (New York, 1985), p. 190.

⁹ Alan Paton, *Cry, the Beloved Country* (London, 1948), p. 42.

RUSSELL VANDENBROUCKE

Fathers and Son:
"Master Harold" . . . and the boys

"Trash is what people is dat puts dirt on de head er dey fren's en makes 'em ashamed." . . .

It was fifteen minutes before I could work myself up to go and humble myself to a nigger; but I done it, and I warn't ever sorry for it afterward, neither. I didn't do him no more mean tricks, and I wouldn't done that one if I'd 'a' knowed it would make him feel that way.   —MARK TWAIN

Fugard's next play was a five-minute mime commissioned by the Actors Theatre of Louisville for its annual festival of new plays. It was part of *The American Project,* an evening of short plays on America by foreign playwrights. *The Drummer* captures a moment in the life of an urban bum who discovers a pair of drumsticks as he works his way through a pile of rubbish. Surrounded by the noises of the city, he begins to tap the sticks idly on a trashcan lid. As he becomes engrossed in his drumming, he first empties the can, then turns it upside down to make it reverberate even more. Holding his drumsticks at the ready, "He chooses a direction and sets off to take on the city. He has discovered it is full of drums . . . and he has got drumsticks." Fugard's only other extended use of mime occurs at the beginning and end of *The Island.*

In an introductory note to his three pages of stage directions, Fugard describes the model for *The Drummer,* whom Fugard had seen only once, in Times Square: "He was moving effortlessly through the congested traffic beating out a tattoo with a pair of drumsticks on anything that came to hand. . . . He wasn't begging. In fact in his relationship to the world around him the roles of giver and receiver seemed to be just the reverse. He was very joyous . . . defiantly so! . . . and seemed to have a sense of himself as being extravagantly free."

Fugard completed the play in 1979. In his undated cover letter to ElizaBeth King, Louisville's literary manager, he wrote, "Enclosed with this letter is a response to the intimidating invitation from the Actors Theatre which reached me via my good friend and agent, Esther Sherman. If it means nothing to you please do not hesitate to crumple it up and throw it into your wastepaper basket. I will be the first to understand. . . . My mandate to the actor is simple . . . find two drumsticks and with the help of those find first joy, and then courage."

Fugard's uncertainty about the piece, which he considered calling *The Beginning,* proved to be unfounded. *The Drummer* was first performed by Dierk Toporzysek, under the direction of Michael Hankins, on February 27, 1980. In contrast to *Dimetos,* Fugard's only other commission, the reviews were largely enthusiastic. *The Drummer* was generally considered the best playlet in *The America Project.* It is the only one of his plays Fugard has never seen performed.

Asked if the exuberance of *The Drummer* marked a new direction in his writing, Fugard replied, "I think that actually from now on all I'm interested in is what I can celebrate. I've dealt with my pain. I've dealt with the misery of my country as much as I can. Now I'm just going to laugh and laugh and laugh and laugh." His prediction proved to be half right: In his next play, *"Master Harold" . . . and the boys,* he continued to probe his own pain, more autobiographically than ever before, but he did so with more humor and laughter than in any previous work.

For fifteen years Fugard's mother had employed a man named Sam Semela at her Jubilee Boarding House and at the St. George's Park Tea Room. Fugard was especially fond of Semela, "But there was an ambivalence in my relationship with him: a love-hate thing. I couldn't come to terms with his difference. And as a little white boy, ten or eleven years old, I had authority over this powerful mature man of about twenty-eight." After a rare quarrel between them, precipitated by something now forgotten, Fugard began bicycling home, burning with resentment: "As I rode up behind him I called his name, he turned in mid-stride to look back and, as I cycled past, I spat in his face. Don't suppose I will ever deal with the shame that overwhelmed me the second after I had done that."

Semela was Fugard's only friend from the age of six through secondary school: "It was a very close, shared, celebratory friendship—the man and the boy. Him being the man, incidentally." According to Fugard, Semela "radiated all the qualities a boy could look to and recognize as those of a man. I thought, 'I can model myself on that.' As I started reading, Semela started reading. He and I evolved theories, such as one about the shapes of good heads and bad heads, with such relish and enjoyment—things that a father and son should do."[1] After Fugard had finished reading a book, Semela would take it back to New Brighton to read himself.

Fugard has described the spitting incident in several interviews and had tried unsuccessfully for many years to write a play about Semela and another black waiter who had worked for his mother. *Master Harold* finally began to take shape after Fugard added an adolescent white boy to the scenario. In a letter dated October 8, 1981, a few days after completing "a reasonably substantial second draft," he expressed his satisfaction when, "I wrote the last words, a stage-direction . . . *[The men dance!]* . . . and then predictably a period of self-doubt. That always happens." *Master Harold* is a long one-act, but when Fugard wrote that it was not a "big" play, he did not mean its length: "There are none of the resonances of *Aloes*, for example. In fact I'm tempted to subtitle it: A Personal Memoir. If it succeeds at all I think 'poignant' will be the right adjective. It is also meant to have a lot of gentle humor. I faced the writing of that with considerable trepidation. But bit by bit my touch came back and I now even find myself laughing at my own jokes. I do realize that that could possibly be the onset of senility."[2]

Master Harold is set in 1950 in the St. George's Park Tea Room. As Sam Semela helps Willie Malopo practice his steps for the upcoming ballroom dancing championship, they are joined by Hally, a precocious seventeen-year-old whose mother runs the tea room. He and Sam soon begin a variation on their favorite game—Hally teaching Sam. They also recall their comaraderie of the past. Hally turns to an essay he must write, but the banter of Sam and Willie about the dancing championship interrupts his concentration until he realizes the championship itself could be the subject of his essay. Hally's excitement is demolished when he learns in a phone call from his mother that his alcoholic and crippled father has returned home from the hospital. Sam scolds Hally for his unfilial reaction to this news, and Hally responds savagely. He orders Sam to address him as "Master"

Harold, then repeats one of his father's racist jokes, and finally spits in Sam's face. Before Hally heads home, Sam's ire subsides and his fatherly concern returns. He and Willie are left alone to dance together.

As might be expected, Fugard's twelfth full-length play shares many traits with his previous work. He again focuses upon an intense relationship and the impediments to it; happy memories quickly give way to the recovery of the past through its vivid re-creation; characters again play with the language they love; games are initiated and roles assumed; important off-stage characters precipitate onstage action; hopes and dreams are entertained, then shattered; and a character's consciousness and self-awareness are deeply transformed. Fugard's finest work is extraordinarily simple, but never more so than *Master Harold*, whose central action is nothing more, apparently, than a brief eruption between a man and a boy.

Many writers begin their careers autobiographically and become more "objective" through time. For Fugard, the process has been the reverse. In his Township Trilogy of *No-Good Friday*, *Nongogo*, and *Tsotsi* he presents lives that were sympathetically imagined and authentically reinvented, but that were, of necessity, vicariously observed rather than directly lived. Fugard's own experiences clearly inform *The Blood Knot*, *Hello and Goodbye*, and *Boesman and Lena*, but none appropriates the drama of his own life as unabashedly as *Master Harold*. Like O'Neill before him, he uses his family not merely to lacerate it, but to exorcise his own furies. Even so, the action of *Master Harold* has a more cohesive form and clearer meaning than the actual events of Fugard's life because they have been ordered into a work of art rather than a precise historical recapitulation.

Hally is the audience's conduit into the emotional world of the play. His adolescent rebelliousness as he teeters on the fulcrum between childhood and adulthood is immediately and universally recognizable. However, far from glorifying his younger self, Fugard exposes Hally's condescension, conceit, self-pity, and general oblivion to these personal shortcomings. The intentional insults of the climax are subtly foreshadowed by the racist remarks Hally blithely makes throughout the play. These seem all the worse because they are so unthinking: spontaneous projections of his patronizing sensibility.

Despite his cocky, pseudo-intellectual pretensions, Hally takes genuine pleasure in sharing with Sam what he has just learned—whether it is mathematics, vocabulary words, history, literature, or geography. The exchanges between teacher and pupil early in the play establish their warmth and closeness. When Sam and Hally laugh at a common memory, the laugh becomes an emblem of all they have shared. Apparently, Hally has no friends his own age. Although the servant quarters at the Jubilee had been his home-within-a-home, his family-within-a-family, the Jubilee years "are not remembered as the happiest ones of an unhappy childhood" (297).* Were it not for Sam, Hally might have had no happy memories, but he does have one more special than all the rest—the day Sam gave him a kite.

The story of the kite is reminiscent of the reenacted car ride in *The Blood Knot:* a pivotal scene reaffirming the bond between a pair of characters by reminding them of a shared moment in the past. As a set piece, the kite story is as physically and emotionally palpable, joyous, and evocative as any scene Fugard has written. It is also a great deal more than a set piece. Hally thinks flying the kite must have appeared strange: "Little white boy in short trousers and a black man old enough to be his father flying a kite. It's not every day you see that" (369).

This is the only time Hally even obliquely refers to Sam as if he were his father, but the comparison exists throughout the play and has already been implied within this scene: Hally's initial fear of being mortified should others see him with Sam and the jerry-made kite has precisely the same roots as the embarrassment he has felt when his mother wears an evening gown. Such typically adolescent discomfort pales beside the public humiliation he had experienced while carrying his drunken father down a crowded Main Street. Sam recalls, "That's not the way a boy grows up to be a man! . . . But the one person who should have been teaching you what that means was the cause of your shame. If you really want to know, that's why I made you that kite. I wanted you to look up, be proud of something, of yourself" (651).

The story of the kite also reveals that Hally is a promising raconteur. He himself realizes it would make a nice short story, "The Kite-Flyers," if there were only a twist in the ending. (It turns out there had been a twist, but Sam had hidden it from Hally; Sam had left Hally alone on a bench at the time because it was whites-only.) Hally also thinks the kite incident could be the start of a novel called *Afternoons in Sam's Room* that would include other stories. He may also have a knack for yet another form of writing. After recalling the look and feel of Sam's room, he says, "Right, so much for the stage directions. Now the characters" (321).

Hally savors the taste of words, sometimes pretentiously, but always sincerely. His inventive mind is also evident in his approach to his school

---

* Editor's note: All quotes are from *"Master Harold" . . . and the boys,* (New York: Alfred A. Knopf, 1982). Line numbers are from the play as presented in this casebook.

assignment. Instead of settling for a pedestrian topic, Hally's imagination, like Fugard's when he was a decade older, seizes the simple life around him and perceives the universal truths embodied by the concrete particulars in the lives of blacks.

As extraordinary as the story of the kite is, *Master Harold* contains another set piece equally vivid. This time it is Sam's turn to tell a story, and he etches a detailed portrait of the 1950 Eastern Province Open Ballroom Dancing Championships. Sam's utopian vision of the dance floor as the embodiment of an ideal life fills the budding writer with admiration; the idyllic dreamworld of a dance floor becomes a metaphor for a world without collisions. Hally subtitles his essay "Ballroom Dancing as a Political Vision."

The banter over the kite had ended when Hally's mother had phoned to say his father *might* come home. The phone rings a second time: His father *will* come home. The intoxicating trance of the imagined ballroom is destroyed by this intrusion of reality. The imagined world that Sam and Hally have created disintegrates. Hally might have predicted as much: "Just when things are going along all right, without fail someone or something will come along and spoil everything. Somebody should write that down as a fundamental law of the Universe. The principle of perpetual disappointment" (397). Even Hally, however, could not foresee the cataclysm about to follow.

The reverie of a world without collisions ends, and Hally tears up the notes for his essay. His father has returned home and so will he, but not as a supportive, rejoicing Neoptolemus. Hally says, "Home-sweet-fucking-home. Jesus, I hate that word." (582) (*Master Harold* is one of Fugard's few scripts not set in the place its characters call home.) Hally's disaffection is more than merely intellectual, and in an emotional outburst he names a new competition to replace that of the ballroom: "the All-Comers-How-To-Make-A-Fuckup-Of-Life Championships" (586). Sam admonishes Hally, "It's your father you're talking about" (589), but Hally responds with his own caution: "Leave me and my father alone." He refuses to heed his own warning.

Hally displaces the shame he feels toward his father and directs it at a safer object, Sam. As Hally's shame turns to rage, he repeatedly tries to bait Sam, but the older man's steadfast refusal to respond only makes the boy angrier. First, Hally insists that Sam remember he is "only" a servant. Then he demands that Sam address him as Willie does, with "Master." Although Sam addresses Hally's mother with an obsequious "Madam," he now vows to Hally, "If you make me say it once, I'll never call you anything else again"

(625). Next, Hally repeats his father's joke about a "nigger's arse" not being "fair." Because of all the wordplay previously, there is no doubt that Sam understands the pun.

Finally, in a deft reversal of the expected dynamics of the situation, when Sam lowers his trousers to show just how "fair" his backside is, it is Sam who keeps his dignity and Hally who is made to feel ignominious. When he spits in Sam's face, desperately trying to save face and preserve his pride, Hally demeans only himself. Willie responds with "a long and heart-felt groan," an utterly appropriate response from the one character who lacks the facility with English possessed by the other two.

Sam knows that, "The face you should be spitting in is your father's" (641), and he restrains his instinct to hit Hally who is only, as Willie reminds him, "Little *white* boy. Long trousers now, but he's still little boy" (648). Sam's anger gives way to a sense of defeat and of the failure of the promise he had made to himself after carrying home Hally's drunken father—that Hally should not be ashamed of himself. Now Hally will be doubly ashamed: of his denial of his natural father and his betrayal of his surrogate one. He is ready to slink back home meekly.

Despite his previous vow, Sam addresses the boy informally: "I've got no right to tell you what being a man means if I don't behave like one myself, and I'm not doing so well at that this afternoon. Should we try again, Hally?" (655). Sam has done more than turned the other cheek. His generosity and plain humanity in offering Hally a second chance is an act of hope, not just for this black man and white boy but for all of estranged humanity.

Hally says that he oscillates "between hope and despair for this world" (175), but for the most part he manifests his despair. As the student exchanges roles with his teacher, Sam counsels him, "You don't *have* to sit up there by yourself. You know what that [whites-only] bench means now, and you can leave it any time you choose. All you've got to do is stand up and walk away from it" (661). Sam's challenge leaves Hally and the audience some hope, not of the collective consciousness and concerted action suggested by *Sizwe Bansi* and *The Island,* but of the possibilities of the individual human spirit and consciousness. Having instigated a cathartic eruption, it is Hally's choice either to come of age and be initiated as a man, or to remain a boy.

Sam and Hally are not entirely reconciled, but before heading home Hally begins to rise from his absolute nadir. For the audience, the emotional ascent continues as the jukebox, the only visually exciting object in the spartan cafe, comes to life with the Maurice Sigler and Al Hoffman song, "Little Man, You've Had a Busy Day."[3] *Master Harold* opens with Sam and Willie alone on stage, and so it ends as they dance together, a final image of harmony among men. Gliding across the floor, the pair embody Sam's earlier advice: "The secret is to make it look easy. Ballroom must look happy Willie, not like hard work" (22).

The same is true of Fugard's craft in this compact, simple, and powerful drama. Following as it does the severely flawed *Aloes* and *Marigolds*, *Master Harold* is a convincing answer to those who might have predicted the erosion of Fugard's skill and power.

Fugard says of the play, "I was dealing with the last unlaid ghost in my life, who was my father. Our relationship was as complex as Master Harold expresses it in the play. I had a resentment at his infirmity and other weakness but, as Master Harold says, 'I love him so.'" Fugard had tried before to confront the ghost of his father in *Hello and Goodbye*. Unlike Hally, or Fugard himself, Johnnie Smit never emancipates himself, never acheives emotional autonomy, and never finds his own identity. Instead of leaving his own father for university, Fugard says, "I could have been weak enough to decide not to go." Instead of going to railroad school, Johnnie "stopped, thought about his father, and went back. And that's a mistake."[4] Johnnie is chronologically older than Hally, but developmentally younger. In *Marigolds*, too, Fugard explores a variation on the adolescent-adult relationship by juxtaposing Daan's journey of self-discovery with the *rite de passage* of the abakwetha.

Fugard's father-son relationship—both in life and on stage—begins as that of every manchild, but is further complicated by the presence of two fathers: black and white, strong and weak, warm and distant, adopted and natural. The one's race and the other's infirmity are physical "liabilities" beyond control. The son feels the social prohibition against striking the biological father, even figuratively (especially since he is disabled), yet that same society fosters his trampling of the surrogate father because he is black. Hally's demand to be called "Master" is a proclamation of racial superiority, but it is also a proclamation of emancipation by an adolescent who yearns to become an adult.

In adolescence, a son realizes his full physical power at the very time his father's power begins to wane. Because Hally's father has long been a cripple, this particular pattern does not apply. (He never flew a kite with his son, let alone played ball in the backyard.) However, in most other ways Hally's struggle for maturity is prototypical. The innate power of this archetypal father-son conflict is one reason for *Master Harold*'s impact.

It is not clear in his quote above which "weakness" of his father Fugard considered most disabling. He bequeathed Fugard his love of music and storytelling, but the son also "inherited" alcoholism and, for a time at least, bigotry. Fugard stopped drinking about the time he began writing *Master Harold*. And like many children, he rejected his father's politics — not to retreat as an underground revolutionary, but to step forward as an impassioned opponent of apartheid — and adopted Sam Semela's openness, compassion, and lucidity.

Parts of *Master Harold* were written at Fugard's mountain retreat in New Bethesda, four-and-a-half hours from Port Elizabeth. This little village near Middelburg, where Fugard was born, is located in the mountains behind Graaf Reinet. In 1984 Fugard purchased his burial plot there. While working on *Master Harold* in New Bethesda, he notes, "I suddenly realized that the chair I was sitting on had been in my mother's tearoom on the afternoon I was writing about. That same chair!" It was according to Fugard, "one of the easiest writing experiences I've ever had. The actual time involved was the same as for the others, but the writing did not involve any of the desperations and traumas I've taken for granted to be an inevitable part of the process." He adds, "The experience was a painful one, but the crafting aspect of it was just one of the most serene, effortless exercises I've ever experienced. . . . In the course of writing the four drafts I never tore up a single page." [5]

Fugard describes his process of writing early in his career as "pouring it out and taking on a process of reduction," but with *Master Harold*, "it was not a question of pouring, it was a question of building." As an example, he cites a sentence in the first and second drafts that read, "You should have taken his crutches away from him." In the third draft it became, "You and the nurses should have taken his crutches away from him." In the published script the sentence runs, "Then you and the nurses should have held him down and taken his crutches away from him." Fugard explains, "Now that's a radically different process to what would have happened if I had been dealing with a moment like that during *The Blood Knot*. That would have been a speech a page long. Which I would have then had to try to cut, reduce, edit, shift, and I would not have had enough sense to know how to reduce it to just one sentence. Because it is a complete picture — isn't it? In that one sentence, I now work very sparingly as a writer. Almost too sparingly I think, at times." [6]

After finishing the second draft, Fugard faced the question of where to produce the play, which, as usual, he planned to direct himself. In a letter dated October 8, 1981 he writes, "I am going to break a past pledge and not do it in S.A. first. I won't get the actors I need here and I'm also certain that there are things in the play that will fall foul of the local censors." Fugard probably had in mind both the baring of Sam's bottom and the casting of Hally, who must look young enough to pass as a teenager, yet have the emotional range and technique of a veteran. In addition to these problems, Fugard sought a first production abroad because *Master Harold* is so introspective and personal a play: "I've always had a sense that the plays that lie behind me—*Aloes, Boesman,* and the others . . . that S.A. was half owner of the rights. This one belongs to me; this one's mine."[7] Although Peter Hall offered a production at Britain's National Theatre, Fugard turned instead to Lloyd Richards and the Yale Repertory Theatre, which had presented the American premiere of *Aloes*.

When Fugard began working on the script, he assumed he could achieve the same shocking effect without actually including the spitting incident. Not until the third draft did he write, "Hally spits in Sam's face." This moment was also avoided during the first two weeks of rehearsal until Fugard took it on himself and stopped rehearsal: "I just turned quietly on Zakes (Mokae), took his head in my hands in a very loving gesture, and I just spat that face wet. I just spat it wet, and the poison was out . . . because I also went on you see."[8] Fugard himself also demonstrated how Sam should drop his trousers.

Master Harold premiered in New Haven on March 12, 1982 with Mokae, Danny Glover as Willy, and Željko Ivanek as Hally. Jack Kroll wrote, "If there is a more urgent and indispensable playwright in world theatre than South Africa's Athol Fugard, I don't know who it could be." Three months later, after *Master Harold* had opened at the Lyceum Theatre on Broadway, Frank Rich asserted, "There may be two or three living playwrights in the world who can write as well Athol Fugard, but I'm not sure that any of them has written a recent play that can match *Master Harold*."[9] The play received both the Drama Desk Award and the Outer Critics' Circle Award for Best Play of 1982.

The dramaturgy of *Master Harold* is so deft that it may barely be discerned—proof in itself of its skill—yet Fugard's refined craft is present even in minor moments throughout the play. Consider the textures of this brief exchange:

> HALLY: It doesn't have to be that way. There is something called progress
> you know, we don't exactly burn people at the stake anymore.
> SAM: Like Joan of Arc.

HALLY: Correct. If she was captured today she'd be given a fair trial.

SAM: And then the death sentence.

In only a few lines, Fugard introduces the idea of progress, indicates the extent of Sam's learning, and finishes the beat with a joke on both South African justice and the idea of progress.

Fugard's contrapuntal skill is not limited to his dialogue. The rainy weather outside the cafe suggests the gloominess of Hally's mood, contrasts with the day Sam and Hally shared a kite, and, on a literal and realistic level, explains why no customers visit. Also, while the play focuses on Sam and Hally, Willie remains present even when he has nothing to say. Washing the floor on his hands and knees, his trousers rolled up like a schoolboy's, he is an inescapable reminder of the role blacks are expected to play.

Critics, and Fugard himself upon occasion, have noted the slow beginning of some of his plays. It takes some time for the relationships and issues of *Master Harold* to engage also. In the meantime, however, it is energetically propelled by its humor, much of it "gentle" as Fugard predicted, but a great deal of it broad and hilarious—more so than even Fugard has realized in either his comments or his production. It is unquestionably the funniest play he has written.

When his mother died in 1980, Fugard received a warm letter of condolence from Semela although the two had not seen each other in fifteen years. *Master Harold* bears the dedication "for Sam and H.D.F." Shortly before the scheduled opening of the play in South Africa, Fugard asked John Kani to contact Semela and give him an airline ticket for the Johannesburg premiere. Kani, who was cast as Sam, "arrived at the Semela family residence to find all the furniture piled outside, as it is in the tradition of the Xhosa people when the head of a household dies." [10]

NOTES

[1]   Raine, p. 11. Gussow, "Witness," p. 55.

[2]   Letter to Russell Vandenbroucke, October 8, 1981.

[3]   As originally scripted, the song was to have been sung by Lena Horne. After Fugard learned that she had never recorded it, as he had presumed, she expressed her willingness to do so—without a fee. However, the Yale Repertory Theatre would not pay the cost of a recording session. A Sarah Vaughan recording was used instead. Fugard had hoped to use Horne's rendition as a form of gratitude both for her voice and for her praise of him when he had received a Best Play award from The New York Drama Critics' Circle for *Aloes*.

⁴ William B. Collins, "A Master's Play of Tragic Import Is Brought Here," *The Philadelphia Inquirer*, March 21, 1982, p. 10-M. BBC, "Life and Works."

⁵ Gussow, "Witness," p. 87. Letter to Vandenbroucke. "Athol Fugard and Don Maclennan," pp. 3–4.

⁶ *Ibid.*, p. 9.

⁷ Letter to Vandenbroucke. "Masterful Fugard: Athol Fugard's *"Master Harold"*... *and the boys,*" *Yale Reports*, 6, No. 4 (1982), p. 1.

⁸ "Athol Fugard and Don Maclennan," p. 6.

⁹ Kroll, "Masters and Servants" (rev. *"Master Harold"*), *Newsweek*, March 29, 1982, p. 52. Rich, "Rev. *'Master Harold',*" *New York Times*, May 5, 1982.

¹⁰ Joseph Lelyveld, *"Master Harold* Stuns Johannesburg Audience," *New York Times*, March 24, 1983, p. 22.

ALISA SOLOMON

"Look at History":
An Interview with Zakes Mokae*
(1982)

Zakes, it's been a long journey for you from Soweto to New York City, from the days of developing plays with Athol in the Johannesburg ghetto to winning a Tony on Broadway in his latest play. Could you talk about that journey and your association with Fugard's work from the beginning until now?

I met Athol in the '50s when Lewis Nkosi, a writer, brought him to the place in Soweto where artists used to hang out, and left him there with me. I was playing the saxophone in those days. Somehow we got around to doing some plays just for the fun of it and because we believed in it. We founded the Rehearsal Room and did plays about the ghetto—*Nongogo* and *No-Good Friday*. The actors were not only acting, but also finding the props, building the scenery, doing whatever needed to be done. I think it was there that Athol developed his style of writing for small casts in one location. He couldn't write for a lot of people, because half the time they weren't going to show up. And we were going to be lucky to have any set at all; there weren't going to be two, or three.

---

* Editor's note: When this interview was first printed, in 1982, the South African government had banned production of *"Master Harold"*... *and the boys*.

Was that the first theater in the area?

Not really. Before us there was the Baretti Players associated with Witwatersrand University. They did an all black production of Shakespeare's *Comedy of Errors.* That was in the '40s.

Was that the first play you ever saw?

That depends on how you define a play. It was the first western play I saw, but I'd seen a lot of plays before that. Plays are integral to my background, to my culture. But we define them differently. You always hear me tell the story of how my parents don't know what it is I do because there is no word in my language for actor. The closest word is "to play." So I tell them I play and they say, "A big man like you and all you do is play?" But that's because the concept is very different in my culture. It's like going back to the Greeks where everyone participates. Birth, death, it's always a celebration in my culture and everyone takes part. In my culture the play belongs to the people. You guys talk about plays you own. One person writes them. We don't deal with that; we don't have to deal with copyrights.

Anyhow, Athol would leave sometimes, and then he'd come back with a new play. One time he came back with *The Blood Knot.* We performed the play on a hot Sunday night and it lasted more than four hours. On Monday the papers were raving about it and producers were offering to bring it to legitimate theaters, and then take it on tour. It all happened so fast the government couldn't do anything about it. So we took it on tour, Athol traveling in first class, sneaking a bottle to me through the window every time the train stopped. We were appearing together in this play, but we couldn't ride in the same car. We took *Blood Knot* to London and it was a success.

Knowing there wouldn't be many roles for me in South Africa, I stayed in England and studied acting. Athol went home and kept writing plays. Later he founded the Serpent Players with John (Kani) and Winston (Ntshona). People are more familiar with the plays he did with them. They collaborated on *The Island* and *Sizwe Bansi.* And they did well with those plays. John and Winston won Tonys when they brought *Sizwe* here. But when they went back they still had to be registered as Athol's gardeners to be able to work with him. They come out here and win Tonys, but that's what they have to do there. It's how the system functions. Athol has kept writing plays, and I've kept acting, and we've kept in touch over the years. I've done *Boesman* and *Aloes.* He caught up with me last winter. I was acting in St. Louis and he came to ask me to play Sam in *"Master Harold" . . . and the boys.*

It's twenty-one years since you've worked together. Have your approaches changed? Your early work was very collaborative. But now Athol came with the fully written play of a mature playwright. Can you talk about the working process and the extent to which actors contributed to the development of the script?

Athol is still working pretty much the same way. I think our early situation in Soweto got him used to writing and directing his own plays. As the actor, of course you always bring something the director didn't have in his head. Sometimes the other actors have a problem saying things to a writer-director like, "well, I don't think this is going to work here," or "let's try it this way," or "I have another idea." They figure he wrote it, he should know. But writing or directing it and bringing the role to life as an actor are different things. So I don't have any problem saying to Athol, "how about this?" I'm used to it. And Athol is used to it. So it's no problem.

I'm interested, for example, in one moment in the play when Hally is talking about getting "six of the best" on his bum for misbehaving in school. Sam then explains how they beat people in jail. He gives a very graphic description and Sam and Willie laugh. Was that laugh something you and Danny Glover invented, or was it a directorial decision? And what are you laughing about?

Athol didn't tell us to laugh there. But it's funny to them. Sam and Willie have a good laugh. They can relate. What else can you do? There are a lot of situations where you would never understand why people laugh. "People can be such bastards" is Hally's next line. Sam and Willie laugh because they see that Hally doesn't know what he's talking about, he's thinking of a world that doesn't exist. Once you're oppressed, you know of things the oppressor doesn't know. They might be painful things, but you always have to find a way to laugh. Sam and Willie share that.

Zach in *Blood Knot* is very much your role: it was written for you, you originated it, contributed to it. Do you feel that Sam is your role too?

It's obvious people will think that way about Sam. Once you do a role for the first time, people will associate it with you. But I didn't invent Sam. Athol came up with him. And since the play is semi-autobiographical, Sam is based on someone Athol knew. But I knew people like Sam. I knew the situation in 1950. I was grown then. I knew what oppression was about in

1950. I knew all those things. So all of these things were working for me. The character is born on paper, but the actor has to put life into him and make the audience believe him. Where do you begin to deal with Sam? The dressing, dandy thing is a big part of Sam. Most probably he wears cufflinks, his shoes are always shiny, and he's always straightening his tie. Another thing is that Sam never talks about his family. I have to decide why. And thinking about where Sam comes from was a large part of creating the character, especially in terms of how he deals with Hally. My point of view would have been different from Sam's. I wouldn't have put up with Hally's nonsense, I would have let him have it. But you have to understand the difference in Sam's background. Sam is from Lesotho which was nothing but hills at the time. A lot of the men left for the cities to find work and send money home. Many went to Johannesburg to work in the mines. Sam has gone to Port Elizabeth, which compared to Johannesburg is a small town. So Sam has to be careful or he's going to be sent back to Lesotho, and unable to work in the city. He would have been in Port Elizabeth illegally, so he really has to watch it. He feels lucky just to be there. But for me it was different. I'm what they call an urban native, from Soweto, Johannesburg. I knew the Nationalists were in power and they weren't jiving, but I would have taken the chance. They couldn't send me back to the country, because once the removals happened, I was urban, and our way of thinking was different. So all of that goes into finding out who Sam is. Knowing the situation, being there, and knowing people like Sam helps, of course. So to answer your question, sure. Each time you create a role, there's a sense in which it's your role.

Do you think Athol had you in mind when he was writing it?

You'd have to ask him that.

The setting of *Master Harold* in Port Elizabeth in 1950 is very specific. Yet this is the first Fugard play to have its premiere in the U.S. Obviously the play appeals to audiences here. Do you think that's because of some kind of universality of its psychological issues? And if that's the level on which it speaks, do you think it also offers an American audience any illumination of the situation in southern Africa?

Americans relate to the psychological issues, to the young kid working out his relationships with his parents, and of course they also relate to the American references: the jukebox, the ballroom dancing, Fred Astaire,

Ginger Rogers. This play, like Athol's others, deals primarily with relation-ships among people. So on that level people are always going to relate to it. But there is also another aspect. You have to take into account the situation in South Africa. It's also about a young cat dealing with two servants, underline, capital letters on servants. Sam and Willie are older, but they have to put up with Hally's treatment of them as boys. It's like they're not justified in being angry, like anger belongs to certain people. So Hally can be angry about his personal problems. But Sam just has to deal.

Because Sam doesn't have the privilege to be angry?

What black person has any privilege in South Africa?

There seem to be some typical reactions to *Master Harold* from perfor-mance to performance. In the performances I've seen, the most notable one is the audience's audible and unanimous gasp when Hally spits on Sam. Do you think you'd get similar reactions doing the play, say up in Harlem? Or how about in South Africa?

In Harlem, it wouldn't get the same reaction. Black folks would say, "Why don't you just beat Hally's ass?" But it was a different era then. A lot has happened between 1950 and 1982. Paul Robeson died. Malcom X died. Martin Luther King died. It's a different era now. The mood is different. But the reaction is different even in the Lyceum. Black folks will sometimes react differently. Some come back after the show and ask why I didn't just kick his ass. Once a couple of cats talked about it during the performance from the house! One was saying I should kick Hally's ass. But another said Sam deserved it because he should have kicked Hally's ass a long time ago.

If it were 1982, what would Sam do?

Well, I can't say. I didn't write the play. It's Athol's point of view, not mine.

What if you were writing it?

If I were writing it, I know what Sam would do. I'd beat him and suffer the consequences. But again, I'm urban so my viewpoint is different. You know, what people can pull in Arkansas, they aren't going to get away with in New York City. In New York, people are going to fight back. It's the same thing. The Nationalists came into power in 1948, and the same things are going on today, the situation hasn't changed. So for Sam, he'd probably react similarly.

Do you think *Master Harold* helps teach American audiences anything about that situation? And do you think it would have the same effect on a South African audience?

Yeah, sure. I'm sure it reminds American audiences of the situation of apartheid. And anything out here that reminds people of southern Africa helps. But for South Africans themselves, I don't know. Whites are protected by the law; the majority is not. I don't see how they're going to be persuaded by a play to give up their comforts. Athol has servants in his house. As far as whites are concerned, that's normal. Any poor white person in South Africa is just stupid. You see, the law entitles them to insult us, to exploit us.

Does doing a play have any positive effect at all?

To say it's going to change the overall situation is naive and exaggerated. But some plays can illuminate the issues. Set in South Africa, *Master Harold* can touch on the situation without making any openly big thing about it, without hammering people over the head. You just deal with the characters, the psychological issues, and then suddenly it hits you, the whole racism issue. The play works on so many levels. There are also some plays being done in Soweto which will never be shown here that deal directly with the political situation. Kids have been arrested for doing these plays. Their costumes were taken, they were harassed.

Weren't you and Athol harassed too when you did *The Blood Knot* twenty years ago?

Sure, but don't make it personal. It's not just me. Every black person gets harassed in South Africa. It goes without saying.

It sounds like you think of *Master Harold* as a political play to the extent that anything coming out of South Africa is politically saturated. But Athol would disagree. He'd say he's not a political writer, but a regional writer like Faulkner.

That's high-falootin. As I said, the play deals primarily with relationships. But I also agree that anything coming out of South Africa is automatically political. The politics of *Master Harold* is that it shows the two worlds that are South Africa, where a white kid can think of two grown men as boys.

Do you think the play is trying to expose that situation critically?

Sure. But even though it exposes, it's not going to change the situation. The basic rule of the South African contest is that the law protects the white minority, and the law harasses the black majority. It was the basic rule in 1950, and it's still the same today. Everyone knows this rule. No black person knows the constitution of South Africa. Neither do whites. They don't have to. You must understand all the time that there are two worlds in South Africa, two laws. Whites live in a certain area. Blacks live in a certain, specified area. That's absolute fact. The white world is protected by the government. For the blacks, its a different story.

Can the two worlds be interpenetrated?

I don't know. I don't know. It seems it's getting harder. Twenty years ago you could still think about it. But now I think it's different.

The government, of course, would have you believe the opposite, that certain aspects of apartheid have been toned down. If you and Athol were starting out now, do you think you'd be able to do plays together in Soweto?

It would be very different. Maybe the government says there have been changes, there is more mixing. But they are only cosmetic changes. Those changes are not the point. You see, the feeling is different now in terms of interpenetrating the two worlds. Too many people have been killed now. In '76, children were killed, school kids, eight-year-olds, ten-year-olds, young kids. Things like that change people. They look at things differently.

Do you think any of the writing coming out of South Africa has helped at all?

Yes, in terms of educating people about the situation. But it also depends who is doing the writing. Everyone who makes it there as a writer has to deal with the blacks. Alan Paton writes *Cry the Beloved Country*. We have to pose the question, whose country? If we're going to be fair to each other, and direct, we have to pose that question. You see, there are very few black writers published in South Africa. Poets do a little better, but it's not easy. But it doesn't make sense to have only white people writing about these things. The perspective is different. Anyhow people have to express their own suffering. When I write about the removals, I know what I'm writing about. It's not abstract. I know how I was removed by force from Sophiatown to Meadowlands in Soweto. They move you to a desert with no rivers, rees, or grass, a desert, and call it Meadowlands. How sick can you get?

You don't sound like you put too much faith in the power of art to affect the depths of injustice in South Africa. What keeps you going as an actor? What makes you decide to do a role like Sam?

First of all, as an actor, it's a good role for me; it's a good dramatic role. What else is there? I'm not a razzle dazzle man, so I'm not looking to be doing musicals. If I thought I weren't right for the role, I wouldn't do it. So that's part of it. But more important, it's a role in a play that's going somewhere. It says something to people. I take it from there. It's not going to change the situation in southern Africa, but it hits people on many levels and gets them thinking about it. It starts there.

And where does it go from there? Are you optimistic about the future of southern Africa?

One is always optimistic. It can't go on forever. Empires have always fallen. Look at history. The Greek empire fell; the Roman empire fell; the British empire fell. History shows that you can't just oppress people forever. What made the empires fall? What made the British empire tumble? Anybody who thinks whites will oppress us forever is wrong. It happened in Zimbabwe. It happened in Angola. It happened in Mozambique. It happens all the time. You can't go on oppressing people forever. It's got to change.

HEINRICH VON STADEN

An Interview with Athol Fugard
(1982)

Athol, whenever I see you roaming around freely, I'm relieved. You are walking on the edge of what is permissible in South Africa, with a lot of the themes you are treating. You never fall off that edge. And the authorities don't push you off the edge. Nor do they chain you so that you can't continue walking along the edge. I sometimes wonder, is that because Athol is writing in English?

It's because I'm writing in English, and there's another factor. Another important factor, Heinrich. The days when the likes of myself—old style liberals like Alan Paton [the South African author]—were regarded as Public Enemy Number One are past. The polarization within South African society is extreme now. God, I'm not going to make bombs; Alan is never gonna make bombs; but there *are* people who are making bombs. Ten years ago they thought that Alan and I might get around to making bombs one day. And that's when they were nervous. They didn't realize then that we were actually never into making bombs at all.

The bombs of fiction—Athol, aren't they more explosive than TNT?

I'd like to believe that. You understand I've got to be careful about that one. I've got to be careful about flattering myself about the potency of the one area of activity which I've got, which is theater and being a writer.

How often have there been productions of your plays for nonsegregated audiences in South Africa?

I've had to change my tactics in terms of that over the years. At a period when the policy on segregated audiences in South Africa was rigid and very strictly enforced, I had to make a decision whether to take on an act of silence, just be silent because I couldn't go into a theater that was decent in my terms, or whether to take on the compromising circumstances of segregated audiences simply because I felt that if a play has got something to say, at least say it. And there were years when I decided to do the latter. I did perform before segregated audiences. In a sense I regret that decision now. I think I might possibly have looked after myself—and maybe the situation—better by not accepting that compromise. But I did.

But do you think you had a genuine choice at that time?

I had a choice between silence or being heard.

. . .

In all of your plays and in the novel you always have a South African setting. Yet your plays and your novels, though so rooted in the specifics of the South African situation, seem to have a tremendous appeal to audiences that are largely ignorant of the situation there. To what do you ascribe that?

You take a chance. As a storyteller one year ago, I took a chance . . . I realized that it was finally time to deal with the story of a seventeen-year-old boy and his friendship with two black men. And it's a gamble. There's no formula. There is no way that you can make or decide or guarantee before the event that that story is going to resonate outside of its specific context. You just take a bloody chance.

Let's go back to South Africa from a slightly different angle. After you've been in a country like America or England, where you can speak and move freely, without the kinds of constraints that are only too well known to exist in South Africa, why do you go back to South Africa so insistently? Every time you've been abroad, you've insisted on going back again.

My answer to the question is quite simply that the little or the lot I know about love, which is, I think the most important activity in life, was taught me by South Africa. I must admit that the moment I find myself outside of my country I can cut through very cleanly to why I love it, why I will eventually want to go back to it, and why I will be buried there. I've chosen my spot.

You've chosen your spot?

There's a little village in the mountains behind Graaff-Reinet.

But why would a man who is as alive as you are, think so much about death . . . as to go and choose . . . ?

Because it's going to happen.

Do you think about it very often?

There's a marvelous few sentences in the preface to Kazantzakis' *Report to Greco,* where in the course of it he says: "Listen, I'm writing this goddamn thing"—he's talking to his wife; he says, "I'm writing this thing so that what you finally put into the ground: just bones, just bones. There must be nothing left." At a certain point as a writer your writing process involves a progressive unburdening. You're not accumulating anymore. You're unburdening yourself. *Master Harold* relieved me—left the feeling a little bit lighter.

This country where you will be buried, sixty miles from where you were born, near Graaff-Reinet, is a country which many people think does not have much of a future. I was very struck in this context by a scene from your new play where the notion of *progress* is introduced, because that's something that Afrikaners are harping on all the time: "We're making progress, we're making progress." And the scene to which I am referring, you will recall, from *Master Harold,* is where Hally, before he becomes Master Harold, says: "If Joan of Arc was captured today, she'd . . .

Oh, I love that exchange . . . I was so happy when that happened.

It's beautiful. But your text: "If Joan of Arc was captured today, she'd be given a fair trial." And then Sam says:

"And then the death sentence."

And then Hally says: "I know, I know. I oscillate between hope and despair."

On the stage its going to be (because my mispronunciation of words in my youth, simply because I didn't have a good education, was terrible) . . . it's going to be "I os-killate."

Great. Does Athol Fugard also os-killate between hope and despair?

Yes, yes, yes. My despair is always involved in trying to see the whole situation, trying to use my imagination, in terms of what can happen if maybe I get it *all* sorted out. In that context I get very confused and therefore inclined to despair. What I find I cannot lose faith and hope in is what Sam says to Hally at the end of the play. What Sam's little moment amounts to, is saying to this little white boy who is going to walk out after a series of very traumatic incidents: "You can choose the quality of the life you're going to live. It's absolutely your choice."

So your hope arises from your faith in individuals?

Yes.

And your despair arises from the total political picture?

Correct.

Do you have some kind of systematic or intuitive vision of what you think would be a feasible alternative to what we now have in South Africa?

I can't but believe that any decent social system starts with One Man, One Vote. I mean, I think that is my first and my last political utterance. I don't know . . . they talk about federalism; they talk about something called the President's Council now; it's all a load of rubbish.

Do you think that the Afrikaner would survive, the white man would survive? That, of course, is the Afrikaners' standard counter-argument to a One Man, One Vote system.

Individuals would. Maybe a corporate Afrikaans identity would get lost, but I don't care about those identities.

. . .

Athol, let's get back to your plays. One of the things that I find striking, both about Piet Bezuidenhout in *A Lesson from Aloes* and about *Master Harold*, is that you leave your audience feeling quite ambivalent about your protagonist. Let's take Master Harold. Here is a fundamentally good kid who went much further than a lot of white people in South Africa would: in being open to blacks, being willing to teach them, to communicate with them. Essentially, Hally was not a racist until he becomes unveiled as Master Harold. And at that point the ratio of good to evil becomes very unclear, becomes very fuzzy.

Hally [is] sixteen or seventeen years old, emotionally confused in the way that any adolescent would be anywhere in the world, but when you also happen to be a South African . . . You see, what is interesting is the way he dictates the nature of the relationship with Sam; he forces roles on Sam; he makes Sam a servant in one moment: "Just get on with your bloody job! No more nonsense around here." At another moment he'll allow Sam to become his intimate, and he will stand in genuine adoration of Sam's vision of a world without collisions and say, "God, that's beautiful Sam, you've got a vision." And he can also get around to spitting in his face, all of which actually just reflects his degree of personal confusion. There is the traumatic experience when he leaves the stage at the end of the play . . . it has been spelt out very clearly by Sam that *you*, and *you alone*, can decide the man you're going to be, which was, in a sense, an equivalent moment for Piet Bezuidenhout when he'd stop his bus and listen to those [black] people and they slapped him on the back and they welcomed him, and he realized, as Master Harold has got to realize, that to sit on a "whites only" bench is to do something as profoundly damaging to yourself as it is to do something damaging to Sam. I just think that the South African experience involves the radical degree of choice. I've talked to young Americans, I've talked to old Americans, I've talked to middle-aged Americans, and their sense of radical choice is not very profound, whereas in South Africa it is, and to the extent that you get poised on going one way or the other, the degree of ambiguity and ambivalence must of necessity operate.

. . .

Is that part of the tragedy of South Africa, that even if you make a clear choice, you can be left dangling, unacceptable?

I am. I am. I am totally unacceptable, a radical nationalist Afrikaner politician because of the attitudes I have. And I know that both within South Africa now, and certainly in the exiled black community outside of South Africa, I am regarded in a very, very uncertain light. Inside the country my old style liberalism is not radical enough; outside the country I've gone on to be an embarrassment because, so far, in terms of theater at least, I appear to have been the only person who has got around to talking about black realities in South Africa, and I've got a white skin.

And they're embarrassed to have a white man speak about black realities?

Some of them can't deal with that.

But there are black actors who continue working very closely with you.

Well, those black South African actors get assaulted, get challenged, in terms of their associations with me and my plays.

Are there other things you want to bring to the attention of the students?

The decisions about the quality of the life you are going to live are yours. As Sam says, "You don't have to sit on that bench. You can get up, stand up, walk away from it any time you choose," and Sam was talking about a white, Sunday bench.

By the same token Sam is also the one who says: "You can't fly a kite on rainy days," and Hally later repeats that line and says "You can't fly a kite on rainy days, remember?"

Ja, well, it was a rainy day.

So you would say, "Remember, you can make your own choices, and yet the political or emotional weather can exercise constraints upon your choices?

Sometimes the weather's bad. Sometimes the weather's bad. I wrote this play, I suppose at one level, in an attempt to try to understand how and why I am the man that I am.

If I didn't know Athol, and if I didn't know the man Athol is, and I'd seen only the play, don't you think that I might have been left with the erroneous impression that Master Harold never could have become Athol?

A play's not a novel. A novel must not leave that question unanswered. A play must answer that question in production. In performance.

. . .

So, you think that the ending of this play, in the production, will leave us with a hope and a confidence in the possibility of a recuperation of humanity?

Yes, absolutely. That's what I've got to look after as a director. That's what I intend doing.

Athol, that means you're os-killating again.

I'm os-killating.

Athol Fugard

From Notebooks 1960–1977

Sam Semela—Basuto—with the family fifteen years. Meeting him again when he visited Mom set off string of memories.

The kite which he produced for me one day during those early years when Mom ran the Jubilee Hotel and he was a waiter there. He had made it himself: brown paper, its ribs fashioned from thin strips of tomato-box plank which he had smoothed down, a paste of flour and water for glue. I was surprised and bewildered that he had made it for me.

I vaguely recall shyly "haunting" the servants' quarters in the well of the hotel—cold, cement-grey world—the pungent mystery of the dark little rooms—a world I didn't understand. Frightened to enter any of the rooms. Sam, broad-faced, broader based—he smelled of woodsmoke. The "kaffir smell" of South Africa is the smell of poverty—woodsmoke and sweat.

Later, when he worked for her at the Park café, Mom gave him the sack: ". . . he became careless. He came late for work. His work went to hell. He didn't seem to care no more." I was about thirteen and served behind the counter while he waited on table.

Realize now he was the most significant—the only—friend of my boyhood years. On terrible windy days when no-one came to swim or walk in the park, we would sit together and talk. Or I was reading—introductions to Eastern Philosophy or Plato and Socrates—and when I had finished he would take the book back to New Brighton.

Can't remember now what precipitated it, but one day there was a rare quarrel between Sam and myself. In a truculent silence we closed the café, Sam set off home to New Brighton on foot and I followed a few minutes later on my bike. I saw him walking ahead of me and, coming out of a spasm of acute loneliness, as I rode up behind him I called his name, he turned in mid-stride to look back and, as I cycled past, I spat in his face. Don't suppose I will ever deal with the shame that overwhelmed me the second after I had done that.

Now he is thin. We had a long talk. He told about the old woman ("Ma") whom he and his wife have taken in to look after their house while he goes to work—he teaches ballroom dancing. "Ma" insists on behaving like a domestic—making Sam feel guilty and embarrassed. She brings him an early morning cup of coffee. Sam: "No, Ma, you mustn't man." Ma: "I must." Sam: "Look, Ma, if I want it, I can make it." Ma: "No, I must."

Occasionally, when she is doing something, Sam feels like a cup of tea but is too embarrassed to ask her, and daren't make one for himself. Similarly, with his washing. After three days or a week away in other towns, giving dancing lessons, he comes back with underclothes that are very dirty. He is too shy to give them out to be washed so washes them himself. When Ma sees this she goes and complains to Sam's wife that he doesn't trust her, that it's all wrong for him to do the washing.

Of tsotsis, he said: "They grab a old man, stick him with a knife and ransack him. And so he must go to hospital and his kids is starving with hungry." Of others: "He's got some little moneys. So he is facing starvation for the weekend."

Of township snobs, he says there are the educational ones: "If you haven't been to the big school, like Fort Hare, what you say isn't true." And the money ones: "If you aren't selling shops or got a business or a big car, man, you're nothing."

Sam's incredible theory about the likeness of those "with the true seed of love." Starts with Plato and Socrates—they were round. "Man is being shrinking all the time. An Abe Lincoln, him too, taller, but that's because man is shrinking." Basically, those with the true seed of love look the same—"It's in the eyes."

He spoke admiringly of one man, a black lawyer in East London, an educated man—university background—who was utterly without snobbery, looking down on no one—any man, educated or ignorant, rich or poor, was another *man* to him, another human being, to be respected, taken seriously, to be talked to, listened to.

They won't allow Sam any longer to earn a living as a dancing teacher. "You must get a job!" One of his fellow teachers was forced to work at Fraser's Quarries.

MSHENGU

Political Theater in South Africa and the Work of Athol Fugard

Athol Fugard needs little introduction. His work is already well-known in his own country and internationally. The political theater of South Africa, that is of course apart from that of Fugard himself, does need introduction. It is little known and little written about.[1] Yet ignorance of it can cause a critic to make serious mistakes, as it did Robert J. Green in his article, "The

Drama of Athol Fugard" (*Aspects of South African Literature,* ed. C. Heywood, London 1976, pp. 163–73), where he writes:

> Drama is perhaps a more fragile, imperilled genre than fiction. In these forbidding circumstances (in South Africa) under the constant threat of censorship or closure, it is inspiring that Fugard created plays at all. (p. 167)

and

> This substantial body of work . . . was done in a theatrical vacuum, with no effective tradition of "western drama" in South Africa within which Fugard could place himself and learn his craft . . . Fugard's talent is at work quite bereft of any sustaining tradition and, furthermore, it must nourish itself in opposition to an illiberal milieu. (p. 168)

The assumptions that produced these statements are quite simply wrong, as I hope to show. Nevertheless, they serve a function in so far as they introduce an image of Fugard which is widely entertained and which it is the purpose of this essay to reexamine. According to this image Fugard is the lone individual playwright of talent battling single-handedly in the "forbidding environment of apartheid South Africa." This we shall have to examine in the light of the history of theater in South Africa and of Fugard's own career.

. . .

Fugard's noncollaborative plays i.e. excluding *Sizwe Banzi* and *The Island,*[2] taken together show the human effects of migrant labor (obliquely in *Nongogo*), racial classification (*The Blood Knot, Statements*), the Group Areas Act (*Boesman and Lena*) and the Immorality Act (*Statements*). Apart from the early play, *Nongogo,* Fugard has chosen to deal with explicitly racial legislation. By showing the human effects of such legislation he has effectively demonstrated its inhuman nature. Fugard's achievement in this respect is considerable. No one can surely doubt his commitment to the eradication of racial segregation of the kind these plays reflect. The point, though, is that there is no depiction in these plays of other more fundamentally oppressive aspects of the apartheid system. For instance, the dumping of reservoirs of cheap black labor in the undeveloped and unsustaining veldt and the inability of a few white and black individuals to love each other and marry, though both deplorable, are not to be compared in terms of human loss and misery. The first is absolutely central to the lives of the majority of South Africans, the latter on their fringes. In these plays Fugard's opposition to apartheid confines itself to an indictment of racialism, but not of the exploitative and destructive nature of capitalism as it operates in South Africa. The effect of emphasizing the former is to obscure the latter, especially when a playwright's work can command an audience in the capitalist countries whose ruling classes reap the superprofit the creation of such labor reservoirs, to name but one example, produces.

Then, if the legislation the effects of which Fugard examines in these plays shows selectivity, so do the human reactions to them.

As Ursula Edmans accurately observes, in Fugard's plays, his characters "tend to emerge with immense dignity. Life may be protracted misery and pain, but, somehow, one can, and must, make at least a gesture of defiance." "Stoic endurance" is the key note. Momentary escape from the situation in dreams and charade characterize *The Blood Knot*. In *Statements* love transcends for pitifully short moments the reality of the lovers' situation. But, by and large, beyond endurance there is little more than "a gesture of defiance."

But South African history testifies to the daily struggles of the oppressed majority. There have been and still are strikes, boycotts, uprisings, sabotage, urban guerilla actions, passive resistance, stonings, killings, creativity, music, dance, protest literature and journalism, political theater, poems and recitations, political parties and associations—all manner of struggle. Yet where in Fugard's work is any of this? Compare, for instance, the battle of the people of Crossroads to resist removal with the behavior of Boesman and Lena.[3] Again, therefore, Fugard's portrayal of "the human condition" in South Africa is partial in both senses.

Some aspects of Fugard's ideology have been well identified by the South African writer and critic, Lewis Nkosi, whose criticism of Fugard's first three plays deserves to be better known.[4] He notes that in *The Blood Knot* Zach, the "black" brother, "lives only on the physical or sensual level and has no intellectual equipment of any sort. This brings him very nearly on the level of the subhuman." This element returns much later in *Statements* in the following interchange between Errol, a "Colored," and Frieda, a white, on how they would spend 43¢ if it was all they had:

MAN: Ten cents for bread . . . that would last the whole day . . . ten cents for cooldrink.

WOMAN: Buy milk.

MAN: No. When we're thirsty we drink cooldrink. Twenty-three cents left. What would you do? What do you think you'd want? You got something to eat, you're not thirsty.

WOMAN: Save something for tomorrow.
MAN: No. There's no tomorrow. Just today.

The racial stereotype here needs no gloss. However, in Fugard's depiction of Zach and other black workers, such as Moses and Tobias in *No-Good Friday* and Outa in *Boesman and Lena,* factors of race and class are compounded. These proletarian characters are characterized by their lack of initiative and particularly their inarticulateness. Outa, in particular, can only murmur unintelligibly in "Xhosa"—Fugard provided no actual dialogue for him. Incredibly, Fugard has imagined in Outa a Xhosa laborer in the Eastern Cape who knows not a word of English or Afrikaans. Outa, Tobias, Moses—these are the dumb and bereft Africans/workers, mute and suffering, with which literature written by whites and the ruling classes abounds. Even when the black man is educated, like Willie in *No-Good Friday,* it is the initiative of the white priest, Father Higgins, that prompts him to take action against the gangster, Shark.

It is to this early play, *No-Good Friday,* we must turn for a more detailed understanding of the development of the ideology implicit in Fugard's work. In Nkosi's words, the play dealt with "the gang protection racket in Johannesburg townships. . . . An educated African [who] must provide some leadership in the community" is faced with the choice: "to defy the thugs and refuse to pay up his share or live forever in fear of the gangs." But, as Nkosi points out, Fugard posed quite the wrong questions. The choice was not as Fugard misrepresented it "between cooperation with the forces of law and order or submitting to the lawless tyranny of the *tsotsi* element." The population of Sophiatown, where the action takes place, is a victim of both the forces of "law and order," who enforce the apartheid system, and the gangsters who take advantage of it. Gangsterism is merely a facet of the majority's oppression. The real enemy is the oppressor. The play obscures this fact. By concentrating resentment on the gangsters Fugard substituted a phoney struggle for the real one.

Then the nature of the action Willie takes is personal and self-sacrificial, in the actual circumstances quite futile, and not organized, communal or political. The key to this evasion is contained in the play's treatment of Watson, the nationalist politician. It is worthwhile noting that 1958, the year in which Fugard and the others prepared and then performed this play, was a portentous one in the history of political struggle in South Africa. On the second of November, two months after the first performance of *No-Good Friday,* the Africanists left the African National Congress to found in April of the following year the Pan-Africanist Congress.

Watson is the only evidence in Fugard's plays of the period that the African Nationalist struggle was at a crucial stage.

He is presented as corrupt and ridiculous. He spends all day thinking up fine phrases for a speech at a meeting of the organizing committees. His solution to one of the gangster's murders is "to put forward a resolution at the next congress, deploring the high incidence of crime." He talks of "the liberatory movement," "the heavy boot of oppression," and he calls for action and the rejection of a £3 a week wage. He is all rhetoric and no action. Undoubtedly there were African Nationalist politicians of the Watson kind, but as there is no other representative of the political organizations in this or his noncollaborative plays, the effect is to discredit political action and distort the legitimate accusations his rhetoric contains.

The only other character in the play who raises such issues is Shark, the gangster:

> You done me dirty, Willie. You done me all wrong. You went to the police like any cheap blabbermouth to cause me trouble . . . To the police . . . The bastards who lock us up for not carrying our passes.

This is an accurate description of the South African police, but it is given to Shark, a criminal and a murderer, to express it and again the truth is evaded.

Why does Fugard in his noncollaborative plays discredit or ignore the people's struggle? Why does Fugard's depiction of blacks, in particular black workers, suggest a lack of initiative, inarticulateness, an inability to do more than endure—attributes which in reality cannot be generally applied?

A number of answers suggest themselves. Let us restrict ourselves to three: race, class and culture.

Fugard's whiteness determined that from birth he would live separately from the majority, though as a young man at the Native Commissioner's Court in Johannesburg, through visits to Sophiatown, his early work with black actors in Johannesburg and later with the Serpent Players, he was able to transcend to some extent his racial isolation.

As an artist or "traditional intellectual" whose material subsistence initially depended on organs of state power and culture, e.g. the Native Commissioner's Court and the National Theatre Organization,[5] and later those of the progressive sections of the English-speaking group and liberal institutions and commercial establishments abroad like theaters, publishing houses, film and television companies, etc., Fugard is affiliated to the English-speaking intermediate classes. The ideology of these classes was in itself the main factor which prevented Fugard from recognizing in the majority and its revolutionary potential the real hope for transforming the society whose inhumanity and injustice he portrays so vividly, if partially, in his plays.

Race and class together account for the third factor: Fugard's lack of knowledge of the culture and languages of the majority. It is unlikely that Fugard speaks any indigenous African language. This means that, though as an Afrikaans speaker he has had entrée into a language and culture of the Coloreds in South Africa and as an English speaker into that of educated black Africans, the life and culture of the majority, as previously defined, has remained for him inaccessible. His efforts to transcend racial segregation by developing contact with black South Africans were thus in the main confined to contact with educated English speakers in white areas or, in other words, with the intermediate classes of the black African group.

This limitation has had serious consequences for his work. Firstly, it has inhibited his ability to see and depict South African life whole. Effectively, the life and struggle of the bulk of his compatriots are removed from his experience and therefore his work. This has resulted in inauthentic depiction, the propagation of oppressive stereotypes and distorted political meanings. As Lewis Nkosi remarked about *Nongogo:* "Athol Fugard could not and really did not know anything about the life of an African prostitute." This remark could be applied to Fugard's knowledge of the life of the black majority in general.

Secondly, it has meant that Fugard's work, in its philosophical assumptions and artistic practice, is not organic. To an extent, in fact, it retains a colonial character. Fugard has never contradicted the basic implication that he is a *European* in Africa, which is contained in Robert J. Green's assumption that only European or "western theater," not indigenous traditions, can sustain him. Rarely does Fugard indicate that African or South African thought and culture have influenced him, and in his noncollaborative work there is little to suggest it has. While he makes no mention of Fanon, Cabral, Nkrumah, Nyerere, Achebe or Ngugi, he repeatedly refers to Camus, Sartre, Beckett, Brecht and Grotowski as having influenced him.[6]

Above all, it has meant that he has been largely cut off from the great volume of creative effort in which the majority in his own country has expressed its lives, especially the rich indigenous theater traditions from the precolonial societies to the bustling, vital theater of the industrial urban areas. As it is, the repertoire of dramatic techniques, tones and language he employs in his noncollaborative plays is limited. He has worn threadbare the acted-out fantasy or recollection device, to name but one example. The indigenous traditions, with their rich store of music, dance, humor, characterization, protest and satire, would surely enrich his work. The extent to which Fugard has created alone and outside these traditions has been his own choice, and, I would submit, very much to his disadvantage. But, one might ask, what can Fugard as a white intellectual, separated from these traditions by race, class and culture, be expected to do in the circumstances? His isolation is surely the tragic result of the South African situation.

"Stoic endurance" in "tragic" situations is precisely the attitude which Fugard himself expresses or depicts in his plays, and it is precisely this attitude for which in this essay he is criticized. Gramsei calls on the traditional intellectual to join the revolutionary classes. We must call on Fugard to accept the commission of his society and throw himself and his art wholeheartedly into the struggle of the oppressed majority in South Africa.

This more than many artists, black or white, he has done. His production, *No-Good Friday*, quite transformed the nature of the "erudite" theater of the black intermediate classes. First of all, the play was South African rather than European. More particularly, it dealt with the dilemmas and problems of black people in the urban as opposed to the traditional or precolonial milieu. *The Blood Knot* was quite revolutionary in that, acted by one black and one white actor, it dealt quite explicitly with the relationship of racial groups in the modern South African context and by implication attacked their artificial separation. Fugard's work with the Serpent Players, and especially *Sizwe Banzi* and *The Island*, represents an extremely important and influential contribution to the development of South African theater.

But Fugard's involvement in such theater has been only partial and he has shown some prevarication. When theater was segregated in 1965 Fugard began writing for and working in the segregated white theater, an area in which he has operated until recently. At that time, too, he went so far as to attack the boycott of South Africa by overseas playwrights, which he had previously supported, in order to justify his involvement in segregated white theater.[7] Even his work with the Serpent Players [a group of black actors with whom Fugard experimented in improvisation] did not originate in full-blooded commitment. As he himself described it:

> There was a knock on the door one night and in walked (some of those who were to become future members of the Serpent Players). I despaired really, I was very tired after the tour (of *The Blood Knot*) and I didn't really feel like getting involved with actors so soon—it's very exhausting—but they persisted, and I felt guilty . . . so that was the beginning of Serpent.

One can only juxtapose against this the following by Steve Biko on the question of "white liberals": "How many white people fighting for their version of a change in South Africa are really motivated by genuine concern and not by guilt?" (*I Write What I Like*, p. 65)

. . .

Let Fugard therefore follow the implications of his early work and that with the Serpent Players to their logical conclusion. Let him abandon his work in the theater of white South Africa, whether so-called "multiracial" or not, and turn his attention away from London, Paris and New York to the cultural and dramatic activity of the majority in his own country and throughout the world. Let him go beyond collaboration with the black intermediate classes i.e. the collaboration which produced *No-Good Friday*, *Sizwe Banzi* and *The Island*, to a real involvement in the life and art of the majority. In order to do this let him learn the majority's languages. Such an involvement would, I believe, lead to the artistic enrichment of his work and to the adoption of the democratic ideology of socialism. His work would then be of greater value to the people in their struggle for a more humane South Africa than it has been up to now.[8]

NOTES

[1] However, see *Black Theatre in South Africa*, "International Defense and Aid fact paper on Southern Africa," 2 (June 1976); G. Kente and others, *South African People's Plays*, African Writers Series, 1981; Robert McLaren, "Theater and Cultural Struggle in South Africa: aspects of theater on the Witwatersrand between 1938 and 1976," (unpublished doctoral dissertation, University of Leeds, 1979); Mshengu, "After Senyho: People's Theater and the Political Struggle in South Africa" in *Theatre Quarterly* 9, No. 33 (1979), 31-8. See also feature on theater in South Africa in *Theatre Quarterly* 7, No. 28 (1977); and all issues of *Sketsh'*, the South African people's theater magazine, address: New Classic Publications, P.O. Box 3417, Nenoni South 1302, South Africa.

[2] According to Lewis Nkosi, *South African Information and Analysis*, May 1968, Paris, and an interview with myself in 1979. *No-Good Friday* was also a collaborative play, although Fugard to my knowledge does not acknowledge it as such.

[3] Crossroads is an "illegal" squatter settlement near Cape Town which in the last few years has put up a heroic resistance against forced removal, in the process developing some effective agitational theater.

[4] *South African Information and Analysis*, May 1968.

[5] Both Nkosi (interview, 1979) and Blake Modisane (*Blame Me on History*, London, 1963, p. 290), who acted in the play, report that when regulations at the white Brian Buncker

Theatre in Johannesburg would not permit Fugard's performance in *No-Good Friday* as the white priest, Father Higgins, the cast preferred to cancel the performances. Fugard argued that the show should go on with Nkosi in the role, as it was "a big break." In the end Fugard had his way and the play was performed with an all-black cast.

6   For instance, in his interview with Mary Benson in *Theatre Quarterly* 7, No. 28 (1977), 77 H3.

7   See his defense of this about-face in the Benson interview and in the introduction to *Boesman and Lena and Other Plays* (Oxford, 1978).

8   The socialist artist in South Africa does not have to declare his/her socialism. There are many ways of fighting the socialist cause in art and literature in South Africa without offering the state the opportunity to crush one.

ROBERT M. POST

Racism in Athol Fugard's "Master Harold" . . . and the boys

Athol Fugard, the only South African playwright with a reputation outside South Africa, is frequently judged to be an excellent chronicler of his country's underlying problems. Jack Kroll has written that "If there is a more urgent and indispensable playwright in world theater [today] than South Africa's Athol Fugard, I don't know who it could be" (Kroll 52). Walter Kerr has called *"Master Harold"* . . . *and the boys,* a play about the affections and conflicts of a white boy and two black men, the "shapeliest, most dimensional, most commanding piece of work the author has yet done for the theater" (Kerr 8). Although Fugard denies he is a political writer (Lawson 6), printed copies of *"Master Harold,"* his latest work, were briefly banned by the Directorate of Publications in the Afrikaner playwright's native country. The fact is especially noteworthy since most of the plays by this dramatist explore the subject of racism in South Africa, but none have previously been banned there. Other of his plays have been more political in tone, but it was obviously the ways in which the relationships of the races were presented in *"Master Harold"* which led to the temporary banning of the play's text.[1]

Fugard frequently draws a cause-effect connection between racism and the situations of characters. In *Nongogo,* for example, Queeny experiences guilt after deserting her younger brothers and sisters upon the death of their mother; she becomes a prostitute because this was the only way in this society for her to earn wages and eventually establish her shebeen business. In *No-Good Friday* Willie despairs because of the way people of his race defer to whites, but he eventually emerges a hero when he reports Tobias's murder to the authorities. The brothers Morris and Zachariah in *The Blood Knot* are upset when the white pen-pal they have accidentally chosen for Zach says she will pay them a visit; they are so terrified of the consequences of the system of apartheid that they plan to pass Morris, who is colored or of mixed race, as a white man. White oppressors cause the title characters in *Boesman and Lena* to trudge hopelessly from one shack to another, but the colored Boesman and Lena, in turn, are prejudiced toward the old black man they meet. In *Sizwe Bansi Is Dead*, devised by Fugard with John Kani and Winston Ntshona, a black South African takes the passport and the identity of a dead man so he can work. *The Island*, also devised with Kani and Ntshona, sets the individual conscience and rights of black political prisoners against the white government, a conflict which is at the heart of Sophocles' *Antigone*. In *Statements after an Arrest under the Immorality Act* a white woman and her colored lover are arrested after being reported to the police by a neighbor of the woman. The effects of a racist government on both colored and white races are evident in *A Lesson from Aloes*. The colored man is banned, and, knowing he will never be free in his own country, he prepares to leave for England. The white woman's mind disintegrates after a painful raid by the authorities of her home and possessions, and at the end of the play, only the white man, like aloes after a drought, remains, deprived of best friend and wife. In *Tsotsi*, Fugard's only novel, the title character loses his memory and becomes a street hoodlum after the white government abducts his mother, and the action of the novel follows the stages in the recovery of his memory and his resulting salvation.

Fugard places the events of *"Master Harold"* . . . *and the boys,* copyrighted in 1982,[2] in 1950 in South Africa. Historically, this is about the time that the policy of apartheid, long in developing, began to be practiced. It was the year the Population Registration Act, which divided the population into four racial groups, was passed, and it was the year the Immorality Act was made stricter. Communism was prohibited, and Zulu and Indians clashed in Durban in 1950. The play is set ten years before South Africa became a republic and the demonstration at Sharpeville took place and sixteen years before the Soweto riots.

The setting of the play is the tea room owned by Hally's family in Port Elizabeth. It is a depressing setting: "a few stale cakes," "not very impressive display of sweets, cigarettes and cool drinks, etc.," "a few cardboard advertising handouts," "a few sad ferns" (1). Except for Hally, Sam, and Willie, the room is deserted; the characters are, in a sense, isolated. The wet and windy weather outside is a portent of the storm that will overtake Hally and Sam inside before the play concludes.

Sam and Willie, two black men in their mid-forties, start the action of the play with talk of dancing and with the practicing of some ballroom dance steps. Dance becomes the major symbol in the play with the specific symbol being the 1950 Eastern Province Open Ballroom Dancing Championship, which becomes representative of relationships of the characters, of race relations, and of associations in the world in general. Champion dancers do not collide; it is "like being in a dream about a world in which accidents don't happen" (542). "And it's beautiful because that is what we want life to be like" (545). People and nations do not perform like champions but bump into each other, yet as long as the music lasts at the dance, the final six couples will "get it right, the way we want life to be" (547). The characters admit that there have probably been leaders who have worked for "the way we want life to be," and name Gandhi, the Pope, members of the United Nations, and Field-Marshall Jan Smuts, who coincidentally died the year the action of the play takes place.

The beginning of the play is pleasant but not without minor conflict. Sam, the wiser and more comprehending of the two black men, is instructing Willie in dancing. Some natural tension is created as Sam criticizes the dancer for holding himself too stiffly; his dancing does not look like romance, a "Love story with happy ending" (35). It is not uncommon for the obviously close friends to quarrel. Willie is somewhat humanized and at the same time made less respectable than Sam by his being portrayed as a woman beater. His dance partner, Hilda, has not appeared for practice since her last "hiding." However, the overall atmosphere is pleasant, and the pleasantness continues with the entrance of Hally, a seventeen-year-old white boy. His opening banter with the men informs us of the good rapport and comradeship between him and them. His later bossing them around does not seem especially unnatural under the circumstances since the men are employees of his parents. Hally's hitting Willie with a ruler after the boy has been disturbed at his table does not even appear unique or especially unusual, but Hally's rather rapid shifts of mood are symptomatic of the inner tension which is later released.

Hally is established as an intelligent, thoughtful young man. He has been transferring his learnings from the Standard Four class through his present Standard Nine to Sam, who proves an apt student with a good memory. This is demonstrated in a mental game in which they try to think of persons who have been people of magnitude, people whose works have genuinely helped society. Their list includes Darwin, Lincoln, Shakespeare, Tolstoy, Jesus, and Sir Alexander Fleming. Hally has thought about religion (he is an atheist), calls comic books "Mental pollution" (113), and has a generally pessimistic outlook on the world: "It's a bloody awful world when you come to think of it. People can be real bastards" (169). Although he does not mention South Africa and its system of apartheid, as a liberal member of the minority ruling class, he must have his country in mind when he comments on the world at large. At the same time, this pessimism is occasionally tempered by hope.

While Hally has been Sam's tutor in intellectual matters, Sam has tried to be Hally's teacher in matters emotional and practical. When his parents ran a boarding house prior to operating the tea room, a younger Hally would hide out in Sam and Willie's room where he would share his studies with Sam, and Sam would instruct the boy in such worldly topics as sex. Hally almost wishes they were back in that room because "life felt the right size in there" (379).

Sam was more than a friend and mentor to Hally; he was a succedaneum father. As mentioned above, there is a rapport, a communion, between Sam and Hally. Hally's real father, a cripple and a drunk, does not spend much time with his son and does not have his respect. Hally's character has been shaped by a dichotomy of feelings for his father; he both loves and is ashamed of his parent. Once in the past Sam had to go into a bar, after Hally had received permission for the black man to enter, to carry the father home because he had passed out from drinking: "A crowded Main Street with all the people watching a little white boy following his drunk father on a nigger's back! I felt for that little boy . . . Master Harold" (649). Sam realized this drunk was not the person to teach a boy to be a man. Sam's desire for Hally to mature successfully is crystallized in the kite-flying reminiscence. After the episode with Hally's drunken father, Sam made a rough kite of brown paper and tomato-box wood pasted together with flour and water and with a tail of the boy's mother's old stockings. Hally remembers being ashamed of the toy and of Sam as they went up the hill to test the kite. Instead of the fiasco ("'Like everything else in my life'" (349) he expected, there was a miracle. The kite flew. Hally remembers their tying the kite to a bench so he could sit and watch it, and he wondered at the time why Sam went away; he learned years later that it was because the bench was for "Whites Only." When he was younger, Hally was seemingly oblivious of some consequences of the differences between colors of skin. Kites do not stay aloft for long, and Hally remembers his sadness at seeing the kite on the ground after its descent. It reminded him of something that had lost its soul, a parallel to Hally's lost soul at the end of the play. Sam built the kite so Hally could forget his weak father and grow toward maturity: "I wanted you to look up, be proud of something, of yourself" (651).

Sam, obviously the most admirable character in the play, certainly more admirable than the unseen father, fails in his educating of Hally because Hally's ties to his bigot father are too strong. Mel Gussow believes that Fugard is suggesting "that if a man such as Sam fails with his single pupil the idea of true racial equality is unattainable" (Gussow, "Master—Servant Friendship" 6). Blood ties and common skin color are stronger bonds than the rapport between the son and substitute father. The boy is clearly upset when he learns his father has come home from the hospital after he has implored his mother to convince him to stay there. Yet, at the turning point of the play, he speaks familiarly with his father on the telephone, called him "chum" and "pal." It is as though the lessons taught by the black man cannot compete successfully with the influence a white man has over his son. After Sam pleads with Hally not to speak disrespectfully about his own father, the effects of racism come bluntly into view. Guilt over his mixed feelings about his parent causes the boy to lash out at the one who has probably meant the most to him. Gerald Weales feels that Hally "kills the father symbolically by attacking Sam." It is extremely ironic that the boy who wanted his father to stay in the hospital—to stay out of his life, in other words—and who speaks so unkindly of him would change so completely to side with his father against Sam and the black race. It is a blatant example of the effects of racism.

Hally insists that Sam show him the same respect Willie does by hereafter addressing him as "Master Harold." Actually, Willie usually calls him "Master Hally," an appellation in which formality is tempered with familiarity. Hally wants all past familiarity with Sam to end. He makes sure that this will happen by swearing that he shares the humor of a racist joke with his father. Very much like Johnnie Smit's identification with his father in the earlier *Hello and Goodbye*, it is as though Hally needs to take the place of his symbolically murdered father. In attempting to humiliate Sam, Hally manages only to degrade himself further. By dropping his pants, Sam further debases Hally, but Hally's ultimate disgrace occurs when he spits in Sam's face. In this moment, hope for any further communion between the two evaporates, but Sam tries even then to save Hally: "The face you should be spitting in is your father's . . . but you used mine, because you think you're safe inside your fair skin" (641). Still giving Hally a chance to look upward and save himself from the debilitating influence of his father, Sam suggests that they fly another kite. Hally's response, "You can't fly kites on rainy days, remember" (658), shows that his inner tempests preclude a reconciliation between the two. To Sam's metaphorical question about hoping for better weather tomorrow, Hally can only reply, "I don't know anything anymore" (660).

The painfully ironic effects of apartheid are perfectly reflected in the title of the play, which John Simon finds "overexplicit" (Simon 76). The boy's name is capitalized to indicate its importance, and its special aura is heightened by the quotation marks enclosing it. An ellipsis points up the distance—social, political, etc.—between Master Harold and the two black men, called "the boys" in lower case. The action of the play and relationships between characters can be charted to a degree by what the characters call each other. The closeness of the black men is emphasized when Willie frequently calls Sam "boet" or brother. During the first part of the play Sam calls Hally "Hally," while Hally refers to Sam and Willie as "chaps" and "gentlemen." His insisting on Sam's calling him "Master Harold" evinces the change that has occurred between the two and cements the theme of racism.

Master Harold is a boy, and "the boys" are men. As Zakes Mokae, the actor who created the part of Sam, has said, "'Master Harold' shows the two worlds that are South Africa, where a white kid can think of two grown men as boys" (Solomon 30). Hally is desperately confused and more than likely scarred permanently by what has happened. However, the black men, more accustomed to destruction and other cruelties to which the most downtrodden victims of racism are subjected, end the play as they began— by dancing. They dance to Sarah Vaughan's pointedly singing "Little man you've had a busy day" (664). In the dance they can dream of the perfect world, a world free of racism, a world where Master Harold and the boys are simply Hally, Sam, and Willie.

The effect of Fugard's play is universal; anyone of any race in any part of the world can relate to the bigotry and racism the play exposes. We are told, however, that the play began as a personal expiation of guilt on the part of the author. The playwright admits that this drama is "'the most totally and immediately autobiographical'" (Gussow, "Witness" 47) of his writings, and he has made no attempt to disguise autobiographical aspects of the play (Gussow 47–94). He has, for example, used real names: Harold and Hally (Fugard's own first name and nickname), Sam Semela, Willie Malopo, and his mother's St. George's Park Tea Room. His father was crippled, the result of an accident on board a ship when he was a child, and he was "'full of pointless, unthought-out prejudices'" (Gussow 52). Key actions in the play are also based on fact, including the carrying home of the drunken father, the kite making and flying, and the white boy's spitting on the black man.

Regarding his spitting on the real-life Sam, Fugard recorded the following in his notebooks: "'Don't suppose I will ever deal with the shame that overwhelmed me the second after I had done that.'" (Gussow 56). *"Master Harold"* . . . *and the boys,* dedicated to both Sam and Fugard's father, is an attempt to deal with the shame, but it is not only Fugard's shame. It is the shame of racism, wherever it exists and in whatever form. Perhaps the banning of the play in South Africa, even as short-lived as it was, is a telling testament to the effectiveness of the play in conveying its theme of anti-racism.

NOTES

[1] *"Master Harold"* . . . *and the boys* has been performed in Johannesburg before mixed audiences of blacks and whites. Performance and text come under different sections of the country's censorship laws.

[2] *"Master Harold"* . . . *and the boys* was first performed at the Yale Repertory Theatre on March 12, 1982.

WORKS CITED

Fugard, Athol. *"Master Harold"* . . . *and the boys.* New York: 1982.

Gussow, Mel. "Athol Fugard Looks at a Master–Servant Friendship." *New York Times* 21 Mar. 1982: D6.

———. "Witness." *New Yorker* 20 Dec. 1982: 47–94.

Kerr, Walter. "'Medea' and 'Master Harold' Bring Fire to Broadway." *New York Times* 16 May 1982: D8.

Kroll, Jack. "Masters and Servants." *Newsweek* 29 Mar. 1982: 52.

Lawson, Steve. "Fugard Tries a Lighter Touch." *New York Times* 2 May 1982: D6.

Simon, John. "Two Harolds and No Medea." *New York* 17 May 1982: 76.

Solomon, Alisa. "'Look at History': An Interview with Zakes Mokae." *Theatre* Winter 1982: 30.

JOHN O. JORDAN

Life in the Theater: Autobiography, Politics, and Romance in "Master Harold" . . . and the boys

SAM: The secret is to make it look easy. Ballroom must look happy, Willie, not like hard work. It must . . . Ja! . . . it must look like romance.

WILLIE: Now another one! What's romance?
SAM: Love story with happy ending. (5)

Standard accounts of Fugard's life and career generally consider *"Master Harold"* . . . *and the boys* (1982) to be the most autobiographical of all his plays, the one that reaches farthest back into the author's own past and that conforms most closely in the details of its central story to actual events and experiences in Fugard's life (Walder, Amato). In addition to noting its autobiographical origins, many critics have taken the play as confirmation of a major shift in Fugard's development as a dramatist: his turning away—beginning roughly in 1975 with *Dimetos*—from the social concerns that had animated his collaborative work with John Kani and Winston Ntshona during the previous decade and his reengagement with a thematics of private life, often centered on the family and treated primarily in individualist and essentialist terms (Seidenspinner, Orkin). While there is abundant evidence to support both of these contentions, emphasis on the personal and confessional aspects of *"Master Harold"* and on Fugard's withdrawal from involvement with township theater has obscured other important aspects of the play and led to distorted understandings of its political significance as well as of its relationship to Fugard's previous work. In this essay I wish to propose an alternate genealogy for *"Master Harold,"* one that decenters the predominantly autobiographical and privatist emphasis of previous readings and that argues instead for a theatrical origin for the play. Moreover, rather than view it as a retreat from social into personal concerns, I see the play as Fugard's attempt to dramatize the connection of the two and as his effort to locate questions of power, privilege, autonomy, and transformation with reference both to South African history and to his own work in the theater.

To anyone familiar with Fugard's biography and Port Elizabeth background, the strongly confessional element in *"Master Harold"* has been evident since the play's first performance in 1982. Lest there be any doubt, however, the publication in 1983 of Fugard's *Notebooks: 1960–1977* made clear how extensively the story of Hally and Sam in the play draws upon real people and events. In an entry from 1961, Fugard sets down a "string of memories" (25) prompted by his encounter, years after their friendship had ended, with Sam Semela, the Basuto servant who worked for Fugard's mother first at the Jubilee Hotel and later at the St. George's Park café, both in Port Elizabeth. Fugard's brief recollection of Semela mentions many of the events that form the basic narrative of the play: the friendship between boy and man, the memory of their kite-flying, the rainy afternoon discussions of Eastern philosophy or Plato and Socrates, Sam's proficiency as a ballroom dancer, and the shameful, culminating incident when, after a trivial quarrel between them, the thirteen-year-old Fugard spat in his friend's face. "Don't suppose I will ever deal with the shame that overwhelmed me the second after I had done that," concludes the 1961 diarist (26). However shameful, perhaps the most surprising thing about this incident is that its young protagonist-turned-playwright should have waited over twenty years to exploit what seems like a ready-made dramatic plot, one particularly well suited for the tightly structured, limited-cast plays that he favored.

In view of its autobiographically overdetermined origin (Fugard even considered subtitling the play "A Personal Memoir"), it is hardly surprising that critics have made little effort to search for other sources of *"Master Harold."* This explanation may help to account for the curious neglect of a passage elsewhere in the *Notebooks* in which Fugard describes what can only be understood as his first attempt to stage the basic idea that he went on to develop later. The notebook entry is dated September 1972, and, although it is rather lengthy, I shall quote it in its entirety.

> After several weeks of doubts, I have committed myself to a total involvement with Winston and Johnny in their first "professional" venture. First feeling was that the best way to launch the undertaking was to find an already written play suitable for the two of them—either a two-hander or something that could be adapted. While trying to find this I also outlined for them an idea which I felt could be developed along the lines of *The Coat* or *Friday's Bread on Monday,* but soon realized if something meaningful was to come out of working with them it was only going to happen if I turned the idea into a mandate and worked along the lines of *Orestes.* One rehearsal in this context behind us and no reason to think I'm mad to try to work like this with them, in the limited time at our disposal—around five weeks to a date at The Space, October 8.
>
> Spent half the first rehearsal outlining, explaining and justifying the method. Told them something about Orestes—the holy actor as opposed to the courtesan actor—truth versus pretense—the "poor" theater as opposed to the "rich" theater, etc. They understood and responded with serious excitement to my rather jumbled exposition. Then applied ourselves to the "idea."
>
> The image I presented to Johnny and Winston was three or four tables and chairs representing the lounge of a local hotel, crowded with a type of arrogant and self-satisfied white student being served by two black waiters. Time—Saturday night; structure—the two of them, waiters, in the lounge before the arrival of the first customer, then the crescendo of activity and

tensions to the climax of "last orders please"; and finally, the two of them alone again, as they tidy up and come to terms with another day in their lives.

Stripped away externals—red-nosed characterization, effects (hundreds of bottles and glasses), orders—in an effort to find our basic challenge. Decided that this consisted of one table, one chair and their relationship to it as "the servant." Obviously the table and chair (empty) is a symbol of whiteness; they are black. A white master symbol–black servant relationship.

First exploration: prepare and place the table and chair, and then wait. Just wait. Winston placed the table and chair, and waited. Johnny took over and waited. Winston took over, and waited. Johnny took over and waited—finally Johnny replaced the table and chair.

Then analyzed subtext experiences. Gratifyingly rich. Their individual relationships to the table and chair—subordinate, resentful, dependent.

The questions provoked in Johnny by this waiting—who am I? Where am I? Who is where? The mask and the face behind the mask. The ontological dilemma arising out of "role" playing. (201–02)

Several salient features of this passage deserve mention. First, the improvisational exercise described here is clearly recognizable as an early version of *"Master Harold"* "stripped away," in Fugard's phrase, to its basic dramatic form. Second, the workshop exercise does not depend on Fugard's biography or, for that matter, on any information about the characters other than their race and occupation. They have no names, no individual psychology. Their roles are structurally determined by social relations of dominance and subordination. Third, the exercise involves only two actors, both of them black. The position potentially occupied by the third (white) actor is here taken by an empty chair. Finally, to the extent that the exercise can be understood as a "source" for the play, that source is (1) theatrical rather than personal, and (2) located at the precise moment of Fugard's commitment to "total involvement" with black actors and township theater. To ignore these two facts in talking about the finished play is to provide only a limited analysis of its significance and its place in Fugard's career.

The juxtaposition of these two passages from the *Notebooks* highlights in particularly dramatic fashion two alternate ways of thinking about the play. One (corresponding roughly to the 1961 entry) focuses on Hally as protagonist and emphasizes thematic elements carried by the play's spoken text: Hally's coming of age, his search for a father, his temptation by the vision of a world without collisions, his cruel rejection of Sam, and his apparent final embracing of racist ideology. In this reading, the play is about white racism and white guilt. Sam and, to a lesser extent, Willie function as foils to Hally's warped transformation of himself into a replica of his disabled father. The alternate reading (corresponding roughly to the 1972 entry) focuses on Sam and Willie as a collective protagonist and emphasizes thematic elements carried by the play's staging rather than its spoken text. In this reading the play is about black labor and black cultural life. Hally functions ironically as a catalyst that brings about the transformation of Willie and, to a lesser extent, Sam into their ideal selves.

Obviously, neither of these two interpretations entirely excludes the other. Both are possible and, indeed, available in the play. Yet there is a distinct difference in emphasis between them; or, one might say, there is a difference with respect to the question of figure and ground. Is Hally the figure, and Sam and Willie the background against which we observe Hally's flounderings? Or are Sam and Willie the figures, and Hally the ground (the empty chair) against which we observe their struggle to lead lives of dignity? Most readings of the play privilege the first approach; from this perspective the play is rightly titled *"Master Harold"... and the boys*. At the risk of overcorrecting what I regard as a racial bias in this perspective, I propose to reverse the emphasis and think of the play as *"The boys"... and Master Harold*.

The play opens on a scene of black labor. Willie, "on his knees, mopping down the floor with a bucket of water and a rag" (1), performs the physical work consistent with his role throughout the play as uneducated manual laborer. Sam, more ambiguously situated, wears his waiter's coat to indicate that he is "on duty," but also pages through a comic book. More educated than Willie, he takes advantage of a lull in the work routine to perform a kind of intellectual labor—reading. It is important to recognize that, with the exception of two distinct interludes in the action, which I shall discuss below, Sam and Willie continue to work throughout the play: cleaning, polishing, stacking chairs, waiting on Hally, helping him with his homework, answering the telephone, tidying up, and so on. If the audience focuses on Hally during the long middle section of the play, it may not notice this work, which, since most of it is nonverbal, is largely invisible in the text, and may remain so on the stage as well. Only at the end of the play, after Sam removes his waiter's jacket, does the work day end and something other than work get performed.

Structurally, the play has three main sections: a prelude when Sam and Willie are alone on stage; a long middle section when Hally is on stage, storming around and "bumping" into people and things; and a brief postlude when Sam and Willie are again alone together. In the opening scene, although Hally is absent, his presence is marked by the single table and chair prepared for his arrival. As in the 1972 workshop exercise, the empty chair is a symbol of white power and privilege. Thematically, it is linked to the "Whites Only" bench in the kite-flying episode, whose significance Hally conveniently overlooks as he thinks of turning this incident into a short story. The chair is an important index of social power within the play as well. At the café only Hally is allowed to sit down; Sam and Willie must either stand or kneel. The only times that either of the two men is permitted to sit, lie, or stand on a chair occur during the two interludes, when the play moves from the "white" space of the café (the real time of the play's action) to the "black" space of the servants' quarters at the Jubilee Hotel (a flashback to the past) and the finals of the Eastern Province Open Ballroom Dancing Championships (a flash-forward to the future).

If standing is the posture of servitude for Sam and Willie, we can better appreciate the significance of ballroom dancing in their lives. Since they are not permitted to sit down on the job, dancing and dance practice are a way not only of providing a welcome relief from the tedium of their work but also of transforming the enforced posture of subordination into a mode of creative and liberating movement. Hence the importance of the play's first significant action, when Willie rises from his knees, thinks for a moment, and then begins awkwardly to practice the quickstep. In a sense, the thematic pattern of the entire play is contained in this single nonverbal moment, not the least important aspect of which is Willie's short pause to reflect. By the end of the play, of course, Willie will have learned to think more clearly, especially about his relationship with Hilda. Just as dancing is a means of transforming the obligation to stand into a form of creative self-expression, so the fact that the two men rehearse European dance steps like the quickstep can be understood as their way of transforming and appropriating white cultural hegemony for black cultural purposes. Dancing is thus much more than a sentimental metaphor for social and political harmony, the "world without collisions" of Hally's homework assignment. It is also a form of disciplined social practice that has specific cultural meaning within the black community. In its combination of European forms with local township traditions, it is also a figure for the nonracial society of the future that is glimpsed in the play's closing moments. To exclude oneself from the dance is to refuse participation in this vision of the future. Hally can sit, but he won't dance.

Once Hally enters, the quality of interaction among the three characters changes radically. Hally becomes the center of attention, introducing his own selfish concerns: schoolwork, a messy Oedipal relation to his parents, and a lively if undisciplined literary curiosity. Along with his pseudo-intellectual arrogance and condescension, however, he brings a measure of genuine affection for Sam and Willie, based on their shared history of knocking about the back rooms of the Jubilee Boarding House when Hally was a young boy. This rough affection is evident to some extent in the "men of magnitude" game that Sam and Hally play together, in which each challenges the other's memory and historical judgment.

The friendship between the two men and Hally is most evident, however, in the play's first interlude (297–379), a memory sequence in which Sam and Willie reenact scenes from the past as recalled by Hally. During this sequence the staging of the play changes from static dialogue (the "men of magnitude" game) to pantomime and physical comedy. Interestingly it is Willie, the most physical of the three, who initiates the new theatrical manner by knocking on the table and imitating the voice of Hally's mother. Although at first he fails to understand Willie's invitation to play, Hally soon begins to laugh along with the others and join in their dramatic recreation of the past. Together the three "boys" transform the white tea room into the black servants' quarters at the Jubilee Hotel, rearranging chairs so that Sam and Willie now have beds. Willie lies down, and Sam sits. Age difference and racial hierarchy are temporarily suspended, at least to some extent. Though all three participate in the dramatic recreation, Hally quickly takes over and begins issuing "stage directions" (321) to the men, revealing a precocious dramaturgical ability that links him once again to Fugard. As the interlude continues, Hally shifts the focus of his reminiscence from the hotel to the kite-flying episode, in which Sam's role as father surrogate is clearly evident. Just as Hally is struggling to grasp the significance of this incident—especially of its ending—the telephone rings, and Hally is plunged back into the sordid reality of his family history.

The second interlude (478–556) is again preceded by a debate between Sam and Hally, this time over the nature of art and the importance of beauty. When Hally refuses to admit that ballroom dancing could be anything other than "entertainment," Sam responds by instancing the regional dance championships for which Willie has been preparing. Again, however, it is Willie who inaugurates the shift in theatrical mode when, imitating the master of ceremonies, he announces in a loud voice, "Mr. Elijah Gladman Guzana and his Orchestral Jazzonions" (488). What follows resembles the first interlude, in that the white tea room is again transformed into a "black" space in which Sam and Willie are at home and in which pantomime and physical comedy predominate. But there are several important differences between the two scenes. For one thing, the second interlude looks ahead to the future rather than back to the past. It thus partakes of the play's general utopian thrust toward a better social order. Another important difference lies in the fact that it is Sam, not Hally, who directs the imaginative production. Hally is now the audience for a dramatic scene that Sam and Willie stage without his help, and, although at one point he speaks of "pool[ing] our combined imaginations" (532), his contribution to this effort is negligible. He has another, more selfish reason, of course, for urging them on, since he has realized that he can use the description of the dance finals to fulfill his homework assignment. As in the first interlude, however, Hally gets caught up in the dream of possibility that Sam offers to him, only to have this vision shattered by a telephone call just as he is struggling to grasp its significance.

The final movement of the play, leading up to the spitting scene, displays Hally at his ugliest, as he rejects his father surrogate and chooses instead to identify with the worst aspects of his natural father. Rather than trace Hally's thoughtless retreat into racism, however, it is more instructive to focus on Sam and Willie and on the transformation that they undergo at the end of the play. The transformation is most evident in Willie, who intervenes to stop Sam from hitting Hally and who renounces his own domestic violence toward his dance partner, Hilda. Whereas Hally refuses to learn from the "hell of a lot of teaching going on" in the play (661), Willie, on the contrary, does learn something important. The plausibility of Sam's self-restraint following the spitting scene—and the viability of nonviolence generally as a response to apartheid, especially after 1976—has been questioned by Fugard's more militant critics, who see evidence in this crucial encounter of Fugard's classically liberal squeamishness about "armed struggle." Undoubtedly these critics are correct, and to defend the play's conclusion by noting that it is set in 1950, when black violence was almost unimaginable, or by appealing to Fugard's biography ("It really happened that way") or to Sam's almost saintly character is to miss the point of such criticism. The play endorses nonviolence and goes on to make its claim for black cultural autonomy in other terms, ones that inevitably will dissatisfy some audiences.

Nevertheless, it is important to recognize that the play does affirm black cultural autonomy and that it does so by giving its brief final scene to Sam and Willie. By this time Hally has left, rejecting Sam's offer of reconciliation and, in a petty gesture of racist distrust, removing the last few coins from the cash register. The work day is over. Sam has taken off his waiter's jacket in preparation for leaving, but Willie is not finished. As he has done before in the two interludes and, indeed, at the very beginning of the play, he initiates the action. His act is simple: he sacrifices his carfare home, puts money in the jukebox, and invites Sam to dance. "You lead. I follow," he says as the music begins and "the machine comes to life in the gray twilight, blushing its way through a spectrum of soft, romantic colors" (664). For the third and final time in the play, the white café is transformed into "black" space, but with some important differences. The white master has left, and the chairs, symbols of white power and privilege, have been stacked and moved aside. Sam and Willie dance, not for Hally's benefit, but for their own pleasure. Most important, perhaps, they dance not in a remembered past or an imagined future, but in the real time of the play's present action.

Thus the play ends with an image of dancing and with the recognition by a member of the black working class of an authentic black leader. (From the perspective of 1982, but not of 1950, Nelson Mandela is perhaps the "man of magnitude" whom both Hally and Sam are seeking. Sam's taking off his white jacket at the end of the play ever so faintly suggests the release of Mandela and other leaders from prison.) That the play should end with this utopian image of black political and cultural solidarity, rather than with a scene of violent confrontation, is no doubt a reflection of Fugard's "liberal" ideology, but it is no less a result of the generic conventions that govern the play. What are literary genres, after all, but world views?

Despite Hally's persistent efforts to turn the story into tragedy, and a rather squalid domestic tragedy at that, the genre to which *"Master Harold"* ultimately belongs is that of romance. As Fredric Jameson reminds us, following Northrop Frye, romance is "a wish-fulfillment or Utopian fantasy which aims at the transfiguration of the world of everyday life in such a way as to restore the conditions of some lost Eden, or to anticipate a future realm from which the old mortality and imperfections will have been effaced. Romance, therefore, does not involve the substitution of some more ideal realm for ordinary reality . . . but rather a process of *transforming* ordinary reality" (110, emphasis in the original). Romance, continues Jameson, typically involves a hero's struggle to overcome some curse or baleful spell cast upon the world. The romance antagonist is usually associated with "winter, darkness, confusion, sterility, moribund life, and old age, and the hero with spring, dawn, order, fertility, vigor, and youth" (Frye, qtd. in Jameson 111). In *"Master Harold"* the baleful spell is apartheid; its concrete manifestation is the gray rainy weather that persists throughout the play. Confirmation of the play's generic status comes early on, when, in response to Willie's question, "What's romance?", Sam answers simply: "Love story with happy ending" (24). Love story, happy ending, transfiguration of ordinary reality—all this and more are present when the jukebox comes to life and the two men begin to dance. Indeed, the tension between Hally's "tragic" emplotment of the day's incidents and Sam's "romance" version of those same events can be understood as a struggle between two world views, one that insists on repeating the mistakes of the past and another that seeks to heal and move beyond them. Within South Africa, the political and ideological forces that correspond to those two world views are all too familiar.

By way of conclusion, I wish to return to the question of "life in the theater" with which I began—that is, to the question of Fugard's autobiographical investment in *"Master Harold."* Having argued against the desirability of any biographical reading that privileges the events of Fugard's boyhood as recounted in the 1961 notebook entry, I now wish to reverse myself and propose an alternate biographical reading, one that attempts to situate the play in relation to Fugard's career during the decade between 1972 and 1982. The reading I propose is speculative, and there is much that I do not know. For this reason, I shall present my findings in summary fashion.

"Master Harold" is, among other things, about Fugard's relation to black township theater. Specifically, it is an evocation of and farewell to his collaboration with John Kani and Winston Ntshona, a collaboration that dates from the 1960s, when Fugard first began to work with the Serpent Players in Port Elizabeth, and that continues through the successful international tour of *Sizwe Bansi Is Dead* and *The Island* in 1973–1976, a production in which Kani and Ntshona performed to great acclaim. The strongest connection between this collaborative period and *"Master Harold"* comes, as we have seen, in the workshop exercise of 1972, when Fugard announces his commitment to "total involvement with Winston and Johnny in their first 'professional' venture." After a week or so of attempting to develop the exercise, a footnote to this passage informs us, the three abandoned Fugard's initial idea and turned instead to the concept that grew into *Sizwe Bansi*. Another less obvious connection between Fugard's career and events in *"Master Harold"* is the fact that, during the period when *Sizwe Bansi* and *The Island* were in preparation, Fugard moved Kani and Ntshona into his own house, listing them officially as "servants" in order to circumvent the pass laws and the laws requiring segregated housing. In this context, it is difficult to avoid taking the title *"Master Harold" . . . and the boys* as suggestive of the relationship between the white playwright and his two black actors.

Allusions to collaborative work in the theater appear at several points in the play, especially in the two interludes. In the first interlude Hally, Sam, and Willie jointly stage a scene from their shared past. Willie, the most physical performer of the three, initiates the action, but Hally quickly takes over and begins giving "stage directions." In terms of Fugard's career this scene corresponds to an early phase of collaborative work in which the white dramatist directs his black actors. They initiate the process, but he provides the material and shapes it according to his own requirements, just as Hally imposes his recollections on Sam and Willie's experience. In the second interlude, Sam and Willie not only initiate the action but shape it according to their own needs. Hally's role is reduced to that of audience and redactor. In terms of Fugard's career, this scene corresponds to a hypothetical later phase of collaborative work in which the white dramatist allows the black actors greater participation in the creative process, but unethically exploits their intellectual labor while taking credit for it himself, just as Hally intends to do with his homework assignment. If "Master Harold" is about (Fugard's own) white guilt, the origins of that guilt may be of more recent date than critics of the play have generally suspected.

Here we approach a question of considerable moral and even legal delicacy: the proper attribution and ownership of jointly produced cultural work. I do not mean to suggest that Fugard has ever failed to acknowledge the contributions of Kani and Ntshona to their collaboratively produced plays or that he has improperly taken credit for the work of others,[1] but it is a fact that the success of *Sizwe Bansi Is Dead* contributed enormously (some might say disproportionately) to the international reputation of Athol Fugard, South African playwright, while bringing well-deserved recognition (but little more than that) to Kani and Ntshona as South African actors. The capitalist institutions of theatrical production, distribution, and publicity are for the most part better attuned to private property and single authorship than to joint ventures. They are also racist.

It is to Fugard's credit that, instead of glossing over these difficult issues, he chose to acknowledge and confront them, however obliquely, by way of Hally's homework assignment. In the play, Hally's appropriation of black culture for his own advancement never actually takes place. The second interlude, like the first, is interrupted by a telephone call from Hally's mother, and Hally eventually tears up the essay he had begun to write. In terms of Fugard's career, the telephone call that interrupted and put a definitive end to his collaborative work with black actors came not from any individual but from history, in the form of the 1976 Soweto uprising. It may be that Fugard had already sensed the changing political and cultural climate as early as 1975, with *Dimetos*, but it is certain that, after 1976, it was no longer easy for a white dramatist to work with black actors without suspicion, Barney Simon's collaboration with Mbongeni Ngema and Percy Mtwa on *Woza Albert!* in 1981 being a notable exception.

To the extent that the preceding speculations have merit, the final scene of *"Master Harold"* is all the more remarkable in that it provides an image not only of black political and cultural solidarity but of black theater freed from its dependence on white sponsorhip and collaboration. Fugard's willingness to recognize the coming of age of an independent black theater and to write himself out of the picture adds force to the play's final celebratory vision. Fugard walks away from the end of the play, not in bitterness and defeat like Hally, but in full understanding that his presence is no longer needed. That this recognition contains sadness and a sense of loss is suggested by the words of the lullaby sung by Sarah Vaughan that plays as Sam and Willie dance: "Little man you're crying, / I know why you're blue, / Someone took your kiddy car away; / Better go to sleep now, / Little man you've had a busy day." The song's second verse, however, offers the promise of consolation for this loss along with the hope for a new beginning: "Johnny won your marbles, / Tell you what we'll do; / Dad will get you new ones right away; / Better go to sleep now, / Little man you've had a busy day" (664). Although it bids farewell to an important and busy phase in his career, the play by no means marks an end to Fugard's life in the theater. Of his continued power and vitality as a dramatist, *"Master Harold"... and the boys* is itself the strongest proof.[2]

NOTES

[1] For several different retrospective accounts of the collaborative process leading to *Sizwe Bansi Is Dead,* see Fugard ("Art of Theater"), Kani ("Combatant"), and Kani and Ntshona ("Art Is Life").

[2] For suggestions and encouragement during the preparation of this essay I am grateful to my colleague, Murray Baumgarten, and to my research assistant, Alain Dussert.

Sample Student
Research Paper

Joshua Miron

Professor Amado

Introduction to Lit

15 October 1996

The Problem of Sam's Inaction

in Athol Fugard's

"Master Harold" . . . and the boys

One of the major points of debate about Athol
Fugard's "Master Harold" . . . and the boys cen-
ters on Sam, the black waiter who works for
Hally's parents. Is he, as Errol Durbach says,
the "compassionate father, the good friend, the
moral teacher" (74), or is he a South African
Uncle Tom who has been thoroughly intimidated by
the apartheid system? These questions about Sam's
character come into focus near the end of the
play when Hally spits on Sam. At first Sam wants
to hit Hally, but after talking to Willie, he
ignores the insult and tries to reason with the
boy. Given the nature of the indignity, it is
difficult to understand why Sam decides not to
strike out. The solution to this problem becomes
clear, however, when we examine the possible
reasons for Sam's inaction and the complex relationship that exists between Sam and Hally.

One possible explanation for Sam's inaction
is that he is afraid he will be arrested if he
hits Hally. Fugard sets "Master Harold" . . .

Thesis statement

First possible reason for Sam's inaction: fear of punishment

Miron 2

and the boys in 1950, a time when especially
repressive apartheid legislation was instituted
by the white government in Pretoria. The Group
Areas Act, the Population Registration Act, the
Amendment to the Immorality Act, and the Suppression of Communism Act put blacks on notice--if
they needed any--that they were not to share in
South Africa's political or economic future (Durbach 73). Along with establishing the concept of
apartheid, these laws created an atmosphere in
which "Black violence was almost unimaginable"
(Jordan 123). Any infringement, no matter how
small, was dealt with harshly because the white
minority lived in fear that they would lose their
monopoly on power.

Another reason that may explain why Sam does
not hit Hally is that he knows if he does he
will lose his job. Sam realizes that under the
current system of apartheid, his employment is
contingent on his adherence to the social conven-
tion of black servitude. When Sam speaks ill of
Hally's father, clearly a man who agrees with the
ideals of the establishment, the boy quickly reminds Sam, "You're only a servant here and don't
forget it" (Fugard, "Master Harold" 57). So, although Sam engages in witty banter with Hally and
Willie, he continues to perform his duties of
caring for his boss's child and preparing the tea
room for the next day's business. He realizes
that any report of insubordination might provoke

Second possible reason for Sam's inaction: fear of losing his job

Miron 3

Hally's mother to fire him. As a result, Sam
would surely be forcefully removed from the white
urban area of Port Elizabeth and restricted to
black rural areas where jobs are scarce (Solomon 91).

Neither of these reasons, however, fully explains Sam's failure to hit Hally. Sam is certainly aware of the repressive climate that
exists in South Africa in 1950. He repeatedly
alludes to the situation of blacks. At one point,
he tells Hally how blacks are beaten when the
magistrate sentences them "to strokes with a
light cane" (Fugard, "Master Harold" 29). At another point, he tells Hally that the reason he
could not sit next to him when he was flying a
kite was that the bench was designated "Whites
Only." As Sam knows, hitting Hally would result
in his being turned over to a system of justice
that applies one standard to whites and another,
much harsher, one to blacks. At the very least,
Sam would lose his source of income and any
chance of gaining future employment in the city.
Even so, Sam does not refrain from hitting Hally
simply because he is concerned with the laws or
because he is afraid of losing his job.

The real reasons for Sam's actions have to
do with his vision of the future and the part he
thinks Hally can play in helping him achieve
this vision. After being spit on, Sam wants to
strike out at Hally for insulting him:

Transition—suggests
another possible
reason for Sam's

Introduction of
primary reason for
Sam's inaction

Miron 4

SAM: [. . .] Should I hit him, Willie?

WILLIE: [Stopping Sam.] No, Boet Sam.

SAM: [Violently.] Why not?

WILLIE: It won't help, Boet Sam.

SAM: I don't want to help! I just want to

hurt him. ("Master Harold" 60)

At that moment, Hally represents all the whites
who have insulted and repressed South African
blacks. Sam's desire to hit Hally is, therefore,
instinctive and understandable. Very quickly,
however, Sam comes to view his situation in personal rather than political terms (Durbach 74):

WILLIE: [. . .] He's little boy, Boet

Sam. Little white boy. Long trousers now,

but he's still little boy.

SAM: [His voice ebbing away into defeat as

quickly as it flooded.] You're right. So

go on, then: groan again, Willie. You do

it better than me. [To Hally.] You don't

know all of what you've just done . . .

Master Harold. It's not just that you've

made me feel dirtier than I've ever been

in my life . . . I mean, how do I wash off

yours and your father's filth? . . . I've

also failed. ("Master Harold" 60)

   The most convincing explanation for Sam's inaction can be found in the view of life he expresses throughout "Master Harold" . . . and the
boys. Repeatedly, Sam dreams of a life that is
like a ballroom in which finalists dance. "To

Further explanation of primary reason for Sam's inaction

be one of those finalists," Sam explains, is
"like being in a dream about a world in which accidents don't happen" (_"Master Harold"_ 51). The
everyday world--the one in which Sam and Hally
live--is a place where people do not know the
steps. It is a world in which collisions occur,
where people bump into people and countries bump
into countries:

> SAM: [. . .] Open a newspaper and what
> do you read? America has bumped into Rus-
> sia, England bumping into India, rich man
> bumps into poor person. These are big col-
> lisions, Hally. They make for a lot of
> bruises. People get hurt with all that
> bumping, and we're sick and tired of it
> now. It's been going on for too long. Are
> we like champions instead of always being
> just a bunch of beginners at it? (_"Master
> Harold"_ 51)

As Errol Durbach observes, Sam "dreams of a world
transformed by some benevolent reformer" (75), a
"Man of Magnitude." He waits for a person like
Napoleon, Lincoln, Tolstoy, or Gandhi who will
bring the world into harmony and teach it to
dance.

To Sam, Hally is a person who could become
the reformer he dreams about. Throughout the
play, Sam encourages Hally to write. He helps
Hally write an essay for school and encourages
him to write a novel about the old days in the

Explanation of
Sam's view of Hally
as a future leader

Miron 6

Jubilee Boarding House. Sam seems to realize that
Hally, despite his arrogance and immaturity, has
the potential to rise above his environment and
do something about the injustice that surrounds
him. In order to do so, however, he must come
to terms with the pain and embarrassment caused
by his alcoholic father. For this reason, Sam
promises himself that he will help Hally overcome
his pain and learn what it means to be a man:

> SAM: [. . .] That's not the way a boy
> grows up to be a man! . . . But the one
> person who should have been teaching you
> what that means was the cause of your
> shame. If you really want to know, that's
> why I made you that kite. I wanted you to
> look up, be proud of something, of your-
> self. . . . ("Master Harold" 61)

Sam's action, although small, can be a starting
point, a place where at the personal level, he
can set about establishing the harmony without
which all that he has worked for will be wasted,
and his life will have no hope or meaning.

At the end of "Master Harold" . . . and the
boys it is unclear what Hally has learned from
his experience. In the Yale Repertory production
of the play, Hally refuses to take Sam's hand in
a gesture of reconciliation (Durbach 75). Outside the St. George's Park Tea Room, the pouring
rain makes flying another kite impossible. The
final image of the play, Sam and Willie dancing

Discussion of how
Sam's inaction
affects Hally

Miron 7

to the music on the jukebox, is a sad parody of Sam's ideal ballroom world. Even so, there is some hope: Hally grows up to be the playwright Athol Fugard ("Notebooks" 101), and twenty years after the experience, he honors Sam and his vision in one of his plays. So, although the play ends ambiguously, it would seem that Hally does eventually learn the lesson Sam has tried to teach him.

It is clear that Sam's refusal to strike Hally is not simply a result of his concern for his safety or his fear of losing his job. Sam's actions have a larger significance. By turning the other cheek, by not striking out, Sam breaks the cycle of violence that defines life in South Africa. Even though his action seems insignificant, it is a beginning. His patience is the patience of a parent toward a son who does not realize the pain he inflicts or the reasons for his behavior. By acting the way he does, Sam resolves his tensions not globally, but personally. Thus, through Sam, Fugard implies that healing, if it is ever to occur, must begin with individuals confronting other individuals and eventually overcoming their own misgivings and mistrust.

Conclusion— summarizes major points discussed in the essay

Miron 8

Works Cited

Allison, Kimberly J., ed. The Harcourt Brace
    Casebook Series in Literature: "Master
    Harold". . . and the boys. Fort Worth:
    Harcourt, 1997.

Durbach, Errol. "'Master Harold'. . . and the
    boys: Athol Fugard and the Psychopathology
    of Apartheid." Allison 68-77.

Fugard, Athol. "Master Harold" . . . and the
    boys. Allison 20-63.

---. "From Notebooks 1960-1977" Allison 101-103.

Jordan, John O. "Life in the Theater: Autobiog-
    raphy, Politics, and Romance in 'Master
    Harold' . . . and the boys." Allison
    117-127.

Solomon, Alisa. "'Look at History': An Interview
    with Zakes Mokae." Allison 88-95.

Bibliography

Works By Athol Fugard

PLAYS

Fugard, Athol. *The Blood Knot: A Play in Seven Scenes.* New York: French, 1989.

————. *The Blood Knot and Other Plays.* New York: Theatre Communications Group, 1991.

————. *Boesman and Lena.* 1969. *The Blood Knot and Other Plays.* 141–202.

————. *Boesman and Lena and Other Plays.* Oxford: Oxford UP, 1978.

————. *The Coat: An Acting Exercise from Serpent Players of New Brighton.* Cape Town: Balkema, 1971.

————. *Dimetos.* 1975. *Dimetos and Two Early Plays.* 1–53.

————. *Dimetos and Two Early Plays.* Oxford: Oxford UP, 1979.

————. *Hello and Goodbye.* 1965. *Boesman and Lena and Other Plays.* 171–235.

————. *The Island.* 1973. Fugard, Kani, and Ntshona. 45–77.

————. *A Lesson From Aloes.* 1982. New York: Theatre Communications Group, 1989.

————. *"Master Harold" . . . and the Boys.* New York: Viking-Penguin, 1984.

————. *My Children! My Africa!* New York: Theatre Communications Group, 1990.

————. *No-Good Friday.* 1958. *Dimetos and Two Early Plays.* 117–64.

————. *Nongogo.* 1959. *Dimetos and Two Early Plays.* 55–115.

————. *People Are Living There.* 1969. *Boesman and Lena and Other Plays.* 99–169.

————. *A Place with the Pigs.* 1987. *Playland and A Place with the Pigs.* 50–100.

————. *Playland. Playland and A Place with the Pigs.* 1–47.

————. *Playland and A Place with the Pigs.* New York: Theatre Communications Group, 1993.

————. *The Road to Mecca.* (Suggested by the Life and Work of Helen Martins of New Bethesday). 1985. New York: Theatre Communications Group, 1988.

————. *Sizwe Bansi Is Dead.* 1972. Fugard, Kani, and Ntshona. 1–44.

————. *Statements after an Arrest under the Immorality Act.* 1974. Fugard, Kani, and Ntshona. 79–108.

————, ed. *Three Port Elizabeth Plays.* London: Oxford, 1974.

————. *The Township Plays.* Ed. Dennis Walder. Oxford: Oxford UP, 1993.

————. *Valley Song.* New York: Theatre Communications Group, 1996.

————, John Kani, and Winston Ntshona. *Statements: Sizwe Bansi Is Dead, The Island, Statements after an Arrest under the Immorality Act.* New York: Theatre Communications Group, 1986.

SCREENPLAYS

Fugard, Athol. *The Occupation. Ten One Act Plays.* Ed. Cosmo Pieterse. New York: Humanities, 1968. 255–93.
————. "*The Occupation:* A Script for Camera." *Contrast* 2.4 (1964): 57–93.
————, and Ross Devenish. *Marigolds in August and The Guest: Two Screenplays.* New York: Theatre Communications Group, 1992.

DIARIES

Fugard, Athol. *Cousins: A Memoir.* New York: Theatre Communications Group, 1997.
————. *Notebooks 1960–1977.* Ed. Mary Benson. New York: Knopf, 1984.

NOVELS

Fugard, Athol. *Tsotsi.* 1980. New York: Viking-Penguin, 1983.

ESSAYS AND SPEECHES

Fugard, Athol. "Athol Fugard's Notebooks." *New Classic* 3.4 (1971): 66–82.
————. "Drama of P. E.'s Night School for African Adults." *Evening Post* 18 June 1954: n.pag.
————. "Fugard on Acting, Actors on Fugard." *Theatre Quarterly* 28 (1977–78): 83–87.
————. "Fugard on Fugard." *Theater* 4 (Winter 1973): 41–54.
————. Introduction. *Three Port Elizabeth Plays.* New York: Viking-Penguin, 1974. vii–xxv.
————. "Open Letter to Playwrights." *Forward* Sept. 1962: n.pag.
————. "*Orestes* Reconstructed: A Letter to an American Friend." *Theatre Quarterly* 8.32 (1979): 3–6.
————. "Letter from Athol Fugard." *Classic* 2.1 (1966): 78–80.
————. "Recent Notebook Entries." *Twentieth Century Literature* 39.4 (Winter 1993): 526–36.
————. "Some Problems of a Playwright from South Africa." *Twentieth Century Literature* 39.4 (Winter 1993): 381–93.
————. "Speech to Rhodes University Staff and Students, Grahamstown." *Cape Argus* 20 June 1991.

Biography and Interviews

Alan, Paul. "Interview with Athol Fugard." *New Statesman and Society* Sept. 1990: 38.

"Athol Plans an African Theater." *Rand Daily Mail* 17 Sept. 1958: n.pag.

Attwell, David, ed. *Doubling the Point: Essays and Interviews.* US: Harvard UP, 1992.

Barbara, Jack. "Fugard as Director: An Interview with the Cast of *Boesman and Lena.*" *Twentieth Century Literature* 39.4 (Winter 1993): 430–37.

Barnes, Patricia. "Athol Fugard's South African Conscience." *Time* 30 June 1980: 11.

Battersby, John. "Athol Fugard: The Face of South Africa's Conscience." *Christian Science Monitor* 14 July 1992, sec. 10: 2.

Benson, Mary. "Dramatist." *Christian Science Monitor* 3 Apr. 1974: 9.

———. "Encounters with Fugard: Native of the Karoo." *Twentieth Century Literature* 39.4 (Winter 1993): 455–60.

Brand, Adam. "He Plans an African Theater." *Port Elizabeth Evening Post* 30 Sept. 1956: n.pag.

Brink, Andre Phillipus. "Athol Fugard's South Africa." *World Press Review* 37 (July 1990): 36+.

Bryceland, Yvonne. "I'm Dry—I Think I Need a Rest—Fugard." *Cape Times Weekend Magazine* 27 Nov. 1965: n.pag.

Burns, John F. "Transkei Sets Terms to Free Sizwe Bansi Actors." *New York Times* 14 Oct. 1976: 3.

Calta, Louis. "*Blood Knot* Production Pleases Playwright Who Fled Rhodesia: Athol Fugard, South African, Avoided Being Deported after Racial Incident." *New York Times* 27 May 1964: 44.

Cody, Gabrielle, and Joel Schechter. "An Interview with Athol Fugard." *Theater* 19.1 (Fall–Winter 1987): 70–72.

Connor, Edwina. *Twenty Names in Modern Literature.* New York: Cavendish, 1988.

Coveney, Michael. "Athol Fugard Speaks." *Plays and Players* 21 (Nov. 1973): 34–37.

Donahue, Francis. "Apartheid's Legacy: Athol Fugard." *Midwest Quarterly* 36.3 (1995): 323–30.

Foley, Andrew. "Courageous Pessimist: An Interview with Athol Fugard." *New Contrast* 22.4 (Dec. 1994): 63–69.

Freed, Lynn. "Fugard's Treaty for the Warring Sexes." *New York Times* 26 Jan. 1992, sec. 2: H1.

———. "Vividly South African: An Interview with Athol Fugard." *Southwest Review* 78.3 (Summer 1993): 296–307.

"Fugard an Avid Reader from Early Age." *Eastern Province Herald* 14 July 1969: n.pag.

"Fugard as Director: An Interview with the Cast of *Boesman and Lena,* 1992." *Twentieth Century Literature* 39.4 (Winter 1993): 430–37.

Fugard, Susan. "The Apprenticeship Years." *Twentieth Century Literature* 39.4 (Winter 1993): 394–408.

Gottfried, Martin. "Fugard Copes with Africa." *New York Post* 14 Nov. 1974: n.pag.

Gray, Stephen. "Fugard in London: Interview with Peter Stevenson." *Heresy* 1 (1979): 33–39.

Grigsby, Wayne. "The Cost of Bearing Witness." *Maclean's* 21 Jan. 1980: 45–46.

Gussow, Mel. "Fugard Balances on a Tightrope." *New York Times* 18 Mar. 1975: 1.

———. "To Fugard, Playwriting Is 'Defiance.'" *New York Times* 17 Dec. 1974: 30.

Henry, William A. "Enemy of the People." *Time* 18 Apr. 1988: 81–82.

Hodgins, Robert. "Interview with Athol Fugard." *Newscheck* 21 July 1967: 24–25.

Honegger, Gitta, Rassami Patipatpaopong, and Joel Schechter. "An Interview with Athol Fugard." *Theater* 16.1 (Fall–Winter 1984): 33–39.

Hough, Barrie, and Athol Fugard. "Interview with Athol Fugard: Port Elizabeth, 30 November 1977." *Theoria* 55 (1980): 37–48.

Howe, Marvine. "Fugard Opposes Playwright's Boycott of South Africa." *New York Times* 6 July 1970: 6.

"An Interview." *Momentum: On Recent South African Writing.* Ed. M. J. Daymond, J. U. Jacobs, and Margaret Lenta. Pietermaritzburg, South Africa: U of Natal P, 1984. 22–28.

Julian, Ria. "'No Life Lived in the Sun Can Be a Failure.'" *Drama* 156 (1985): 5–8.

Keller, Bill. "Mandela's Honeymoon." *New York Times* 4 May 1994: A1.

Klein, Alvin. "Adding a Line to a Distinguished Resume." *New York Times* 29 Oct. 1995, New Jersey ed., sec. 13: 3.

Koehler, Robert. "Tough Questions for Principals of *My Children! My Africa!*" *Los Angeles Times* 23 Nov. 1990: F34.

Kornbluth, Jesse. "Blood Brothers: A. Fugard and Z. Mokae." *New York* 2 December 1985: 80–82.

MacKay, Gillian. "Drama of Dissent." *Maclean's* 18 June 1990: 58+.

Maclennan, Don. "Athol Fugard and Don Maclennan: A Conversation." *English in Africa* 9.2 (Oct. 1982): 1–11.

Marks, Jonathan. "Interview with Athol Fugard." *Theater* 4.1 (1973): 64–72.

———. "A Man Who Commits Provocative Acts of Theater." *Yale Reports* 4.4 (1980): 1–3.

Nkosi, Lewis. "Athol Fugard: His Work and Us." *South Africa: Information and Analysis* 63 (May 1968): 1–8.

———. "The Playwright's War against South Africa." *South Africa: Information and Analysis* 64 (June 1968): 1–8.

"On South Africa and Hope: A Dialogue." *New York Times* 10 Dec. 1995, late ed., sec. 2: 1.

Richards, David. "Athol Fugard, Seizing the Light." *Washington Post* 30 July 1989: G1.

Richards, Lloyd. "The Art of Theater VII: Athol Fugard." *Paris Review* 111 (1989): 128–51.

Sarzin, Anne. "Talking to Athol Fugard." *Contrast* 16.4 (Dec. 1987): 64–71.

Tucker, A. Christopher. "Athol Fugard Interviewed." *Transatlantic Review* 53–54 (1976): 87–90.

Vandenbrouke, Russell. "Athol Fugard: The Director Collaborates with his Actors." *Theater* 14.1 (Winter 1982): 32–40.

———. "Athol Fugard's Immense Microcosm." *Los Angeles Times* 23 Aug. 1981, calender: 41.

———. "Fugard and South Africa." *The Guthrie* May 1983: 18–19.

von Lucius, Robert. "Athol Fugard: South African Playwright of International Repute." *South African International* 23.2 (1992–93): 78–81.

von Staden, Heinrich. "An Interview with Athol Fugard." *Theater* 14.1 (Winter 1982): 41–46.

Criticism and Commentary

Ainslic, Jill. "The Fugard Collection in the National English Literary Museum, Grahamstown." *English in Africa* 9.2 (Oct. 1982): 35–39.

Angove, Coleen. "Afrikaner Stereotypes and Mavericks in Selected Fugard Plays." *South African Theatre Journal* 3.1 (May 1989): 55–68.

Arthur, Thomas H. "Looking for My Relatives: The Political Implications of 'Family' in Selected Works of Athol Fugard." *South African Theatre Journal* 6.2 (Sept. 1992): 5–16.

Attwell, David, ed. *Doubling the Point: Essays and Interviews.* US: Harvard UP, 1992.

Ayling, Ronald. "Literature of the Eastern Cape from Shreiner to Fugard." *ARIEL* 16.2 (Apr. 1985): 77–98.

Barbara, Jack. "Introduction: Fugard, Women, and Politics." *Twentieth Century Literature* 39.4 (Winter 1993): v–xix.

Benson, Mary. "Athol Fugard and 'One Little Corner of the World.'" *Theater* 4.1 (1973): 64–72.

———. "A Hunger for Ideas Moves Them." *New York Times* 12 Sept. 1964, sec. 2: 8.

———. "'Keeping an Appointment with the Future': The Theater of Athol Fugard." *Theatre Quarterly* 28 (1977–78): 77–83.

Berner, Robert L. "Athol Fugard and the Theater of Improvization." *Books Abroad* 50 (Winter 1976): 81–84.

Bowker, Veronica. "Fugard: Deconstructing the Context." *Journal of Literary Studies* 1.3 (July 1985): 78–89.

Brinkley, Edward S. "Proustian Time and Modern Drama: Beckett, Brecht, and Fugard." *Comparative Literature Studies* 25.4 (1988): 352–66.

Brutus, Dennis. "Protest against Apartheid: Alan Paton, Nadine Gordimer, Athol Fugard, Alfred Hutchinson, and Arthur Nortje." *Protest and Conflict in African Literature.* Ed. Cosmo Pieterse and Donald Munro. New York: Africanna, 1969. 93–100.

Callaghan, Cedric. "Black Theater in South Africa: Links with the United States of America?" *Black American Literature Forum* 17.2 (Summer 1983): 82–83.

Collerman, Jeanne. "Athol Fugard and the Problematics of Liberal Critique." *Modern Drama* 38.3 (1995): 389–407.

Cotzee, J. "The White Man's Burden." *Speak* 1 (1977): 4–7.

Craig, Randall. "Plays in Performance." *Drama* 111 (Winter 1973): 54.

Crow, Brian. "Athol Fugard." King. 150–64.

Dahl, Mary Karen. "State Terror and Dramatic Countermeasures." *Terrorism and Modern Drama.* Ed. John Orr and Dragan Klaic. Edinburgh: Edinburgh UP, 1990. 109–22.

Dei, Ernest Cobena. *Athol Fugard and Race Relations: Social Dynamics under Apartheid.* Vancouver: U of British Columbia P, 1993.

File on Fugard. Comp. Stephen Gray. London: Methuen, 1991.

Ford, Christopher. "Life with a Liberal Conscience." *Guardian* 17 July 1971: 8.

Fuchs, Anne. "The New South African Theater: Beyond Fugard." King. 165–80.

———. "Toward and Away from Poor Theater; Or, Athol Fugard's Transgressions." *Commonwealth Essays and Studies* 7.1 (Autumn 1984): 71–79.

Gordimer, Nadine. "English-Language Literature and Politics in South Africa." Heywood. 99–120.

———. "Plays and Piracy: A Discussion." *Contrast* 3.4 (July 1965): 53–55.

———. "South Africa: Towards a Desk Drawer Literature." *The Classic* 2.4 (1968): 64–74.

Gray, Stephen, ed. *Athol Fugard.* South Africa Lit. Ser. 1. New York: McGraw, 1982.

———. "Athol Fugard's Development: A Stocktaking." *Theoria* 55 (1980): 33–36.

———. "'A Chair Called Agamemnon': Athol Fugard's Use of Greek Dramatic Myths." *Standpunte* 39.4 (August 1986): 19–27.

———. Introduction. *My Children! My Africa! and Selected Shorter Plays,* by Athol Fugard. Johannesburg: Witwatersrand UP, 1990. 9–13.

Green, Robert J. "Athol Fugard: Dramatist of Loneliness and Isolation." *Theatre South Africa* 1.2 (1968): 2–4.

———. "Politics and Literature in Africa: The Drama of Athol Fugard." Heywood. 163–73.

Grobler, Esme. "Varieties of Dramatic Dialogue." *South African Theatre Journal* 4.1 (May 1990): 38–60.

Gussow, Mel. "Profiles: Witness." *New Yorker* 20 Dec. 1982: 47–94.

――――. "When Playwrights Cross (or Crisscross) the Footlights." *New York Times* 5 Feb. 1996, late NY ed.: C9+.

Harold, Beth. "Susan Hilferty." *Theatre Crafts* 24 (Jan. 1990): 46–53.

Hauptfleisch, Temple, Wilma Viljoen, and Celeste Van Greunen. *Athol Fugard: A Source Guide.* Theater Research. 7. Johannesburg: Donker, 1982.

Henry, William A. "Home Is Where the Art Is." *Time* 28 Feb. 1994: 67.

Heywood, Christopher, ed. *Aspects of South African Literature.* New York: Africanna, 1976.

Hilferty, Susan. "Realizing Fugard." *Twentieth Century Literature* 39.4 (Winter 1993): 479–85.

Hogg, David. "Unpublished Fugard Novel." *Contrast* 12.1 (1978): 60–78.

Kavanaugh, Robert. *Theater and Cultural Struggle in South Africa.* UK: Zed, 1985.

King, Bruce. *Post-Colonial English Drama: Beyond Fugard.* New York: St. Martin's, 1992.

Lambert, J. W. "Plays in Performance." *Drama* 112 (Spring 1974): 22–23.

Lawson, Steve. "Fugard Tries a Lighter Touch." *New York Times* 2 May 1982: D6.

Maclennan, Don. "A Tribute for Athol Fugard at Sixty." *Twentieth Century Literature* 39.4 (Winter 1993): 517–25.

――――. "The Palimpest: Some Observations on the Plays of Athol Fugard." *Bloody Horse* 3 (1981): 59–70.

McKay, E. A. "Antigone and Orestes in the Works of Athol Fugard." *Theoria* 74 (Oct. 1989): 31–43.

McKay, Kim. "*The Blood Knot* Reborn in the Eighties: A Reflection of the Artist and His Times." *Modern Drama* 30 (Dec. 1987): 496–504.

Mitchell, Julian. "Athol Fugard in London." *African Literature Today* 8 (1976): 130–37.

Moyana, T. T. "Problems of a Creative Writer in South Africa." Heywood. 85–98.

Mshengu. "Political Theater in South Africa and the Work of Athol Fugard." *Theatre Research International* 7.3 (Autumn 1982): 160–79.

Munro, Margaret. "Some Aspects of Visual Codes in Fugard." *English in Africa* 9.2 (Oct. 1982): 13–25.

National English Literary Museum. *Athol Fugard: Information and Analysis.* Grahamstown: NELM, 1991.

――――. *Athol Fugard: A Resource Guide.* NELM Olympiad Resource Ser. 1. Grahamstown: NELM, 1991.

Orkin, Martin. *Drama and the South African State.* Johannesburg: Witwatersrand UP, 1991.

O'Sheel, Patrick. "Athol Fugard's 'Poor Theater.'" *Journal of Commonwealth Literature* 12.3 (1978): 67–77.

Peck, Richard. "Condemned to Choose, But What? Existentialism in Selected Works by Fugard, Brink, and Gordimer." *Research in African Literatures* 23.3 (Fall 1992): 67–84.

Pieterse, Cosmo, and David Munro, eds. *Protest and Conflict in African Literature.* London: Heinemann, 1969.

Post, Robert M. "Victims in the Writing of Athol Fugard." *ARIEL* 16.3 (July 1985): 3–17.

Read, John. *Athol Fugard: A Bibliography.* Intro. Stephen Gray. Bibliographic Series. 4. Grahamstown: NELM, 1991.

Richards, David. "The Agony and the Irony: Playwright Athol Fugard and the Agonies of South Africa." *Washington Post* 8 Nov. 1981: M1+.

Schechter, Joel. "James Earl Jones on Fugard." *Theater* 16.1 (Fall–Winter 1984): 40–42.

Seidenspinner, Margaret. *Exploring the Labyrinth: Athol Fugard's Approach to South African Drama.* Essen: Blaue Eule, 1986.

Sweeny, Louise. "Athol Fugard and the Power of Words." *Christian Science Monitor* 7 Dec. 1989: 10–11.

"Three One Act Plays in Programme." *Cape Argus* 4 Oct. 1956: 5.

Vandenbroucke, Russell. *Athol Fugard: Bibliography, Biography, Playography.* Checklist. 15. London: Theatre Quarterly, 1977.

———. "A Brief Chronology of Theater in South Africa." *Theater Quarterly* 7.28 (1977): 44–46.

———. "Chiaroscuro: A Portrait of Theater in South Africa." *Theatre Quarterly* 7.28 (1977): 46–54.

———. "In Dialogue with Himself: Athol Fugard's *Notebooks.*" *Theater* 16.1 (Fall–Winter 1984): 43–48.

———. "A Selected Bibliography of the South African Theater." *Theatre Quarterly* 7.28 (1977): 94–95.

———. *Truths the Hand Can Touch: The Theater of Athol Fugard.* New York: Theatre Communications Group, 1985.

Von Lucius, Robert. "Athol Fugard: South African Playwright of International Repute." *South African International* 23.2 (1992–93): 78–81.

Walder, Dennis. *Athol Fugard.* New York: Grove, 1985.

———. "Crossing the Boundaries: The Genesis of the Township Plays." *Twentieth Century Literature* 39.4 (Winter 1993): 409–22.

———. "Resituating Fugard: South African Drama as Witness." *New Theater Quarterly* 8 (Nov. 1992): 343–61.

Weales, Gerald. "The Embodied Images of Athol Fugard." *Hollins Critic* 15.1 (1978): 1–12.

———. "Fugard Masters the Code." *Twentieth Century Literature* 39.4 (Winter 1993): 503–16.

Wilhelm, Peter. "Athol Fugard at Forty." *Athol Fugard.* Ed. Stephan Gray. New York: McGraw, 1982. 109–14.

Woodrow, Mervyn Wilbur. "South African Drama in English." *English Studies in Africa* 13.2 (Sept. 1970): 391–410.

Wortham, Chris. "A Sense of Place: Home and Homelessness in the Plays of

Athol Fugard." *Olive Shriener and After: Essays on Southern African Literature in Honor of Guy Butler.* Eds. Malvern van Wyk Smith and Don Maclennan. Cape Town: Phillip, 1993. 165–83.

Wren, Christopher Sale. "Apartheid's Children: Afrikaner Writers Today." *New York Times Book Review* 11 Oct. 1992: 1.

———. "A Drama about Apartheid Brings Its Author Home." *New York Times* 25 June 1989, sec. 2: 5.

Wren, Robert M. "Profile: Athol Fugard in Segregated South Africa: A Vision of Shared Hopelessness." *Africa Report* 15.7 (Oct. 1970): 32–33.

Writer & Region: Athol Fugard. Statements. 2. New York: Anson Phelps Stokes Institute, 1987.

THE BLOOD KNOT

Cohen, Derek. "A South African Drama: Athol Fugard's *The Blood Knot.*" *Modern Language Studies* 7.1 (1977): 74–81.

Collins, William B. "*The Blood Knot,* A Tragedy Born in Guilt." *Philadelphia Inquirer* 11 Feb. 1979: 1G+.

Foster, Deborah D. *Blood Knot and The Islands as Anti-Tragedy.* Occasional Paper Ser. 8. Madison: U of Wisconsin, n.d.

Green, Robert J. "South Africa's Plague: One View of *The Blood Knot.*" *Modern Drama* 12 (1969): 331–45.

McKay, Kimol. "*The Blood Knot* Reborn in the Eighties: A Reflection of the Artist and His Times." *Modern Drama* 30.4 (Dec. 1987): 496–504.

Orkin, Martin. "Body and State in *Blood Knot/The Blood Knot.*" *South African Theatre Journal* 2.1 (May 1988): 17–34.

Rutherford, Anna. "Time, Space, and Identity in Athol Fugard's *The Blood Knot.*" *Neo-African Literature and Culture: Essays in Memory of Janheinz Jahn.* Mainzer Afrika-Studien Ser. 1. Ed. Bernth O. Lindfors and Ulla Schild. Weisbaden: Heyman, 1976.

Sanders, Robin. "*The Blood Knot.*" *Speak* 1.6 (1979): 44.

BOESMAN AND LENA

Billington, Michael. Rev. of *Boesman and Lena,* by Athol Fugard. *Plays and Players* 18 (Sept. 1971): 48–49.

"*Boesman and Lena:* A Play That's for Real." *Drum* 25 Oct. 1976: 34–35.

Boisvert, Nancy, and Low Taylor. "Athol Fugard's *Boesman and Lena* on Stage and Film: Problems of Translation." *Transformations: From Literature to Film.* Kent: Kent State U, 1987. 63–69.

Cohen, Derek. "Athol Fugard's *Boesman and Lena.*" *Journal of Commonwealth Literature* 12.3 (1978): 79–83.

Ferguson, Ian. "Athol Fugard's *Boesman and Lena*." *Crux* 4.4 (Nov. 1970): 52–55.

Herbscher, Franciose. "Dans les Coulisses de l'Apartheid." *Jeune Afrique* 14 (Mai 1976): 48–50.

Hough, Barrie. "Fugard's *Boesman and Lena*." *Crux* 13.1 (1979): 29–36.

Kauffman, Stanley. Rev. of *Boesman and Lena*, by Athol Fugard. *New Republic* 25 July 1970: 16+.

Lory, Georges-Marie. "Fugard, *Boesman et Lena*." *L'Afrique Litteraire et Artistique* 40 (1976): 77–80.

McLuckie, Craig W. "Power, Self, and Others: The Absurd in *Boesman and Lena*." *Twentieth Century Literature* 39.4 (Winter 1993): 423–29.

Meyong, Bekate. "*Boesman et Lena* d' Athol Fugard." *Peuples Noirs-Peuples Africains* 13 (1980): 148–50.

Van Zyl, J. A. "*Boesman and Lena*." *New Nation* Mar. 1974: 13.

Wilson, Lundy. "Athol Fugard." *South African Outlook* 99 (1969): 129+.

DIMETOS

Whitaker, Richard. "Dimoetes to *Dimetos:* The Evolution of a Myth." *English Studies in Africa* 24.1 (Mar. 1981): 45–59.

Young, B. A. Rev. of *Dimetos*, by Athol Fugard. *Financial Times* 23 Jan. 1974: 3.

HELLO AND GOODBYE

Gala. "Hello and Goodbye, Athol Fugard?" *African Communist* 57 (1974): 100–105.

Gray, Stephen. "Athol Fugard's *Hello and Goodbye*." *Modern Drama* 13 (1970–1971): 139–55.

Hearhoff, R. D. "Johari's Window, Hester and Johnnie: An Approach to Athol Fugard's *Hello and Good-bye*." *Communique* 5.1 (1980): 41–45.

Peterson, Kristen H. "The Problem of Identity in a South African Context." *ACLALS Bulletin* (1974): 10–16.

THE ISLAND

Anderson, Lauri. "The Audience as Judge in Athol Fugard's *The Island*." *Notes on Contemporary Literature* 16.1 (Jan. 1986): 5.

Benson, Mary. "The Island Where Men Are [Not] Broken." *The Observer* 14 Apr. 1974: 13.

Blumenthal, Eileen. Rev. of *Sizwe Bansi Is Dead* and *The Island*, by Athol Fugard. *Educational Theatre Journal* 27 (1975): 416–18.

Durbach, Errol. "Sophocles in South Africa: Athol Fugard's *The Island*." *Drama and the Classical Heritage: Comparative and Critical Studies.* Ed. Clifford Davidson, Rand Johnson, and John H. Stroupe. New York: AMS, 1993. 241–53.

Foster, Deborah D. *Blood Knot and The Island as Anti-Tragedy.* Occasional Paper Series, 8. Madison: U of Wisconsin, n.d.

Hammond, Jonathan. "A South African Season: *Sizwe Bansi, The Island,* and *Statements.*" *Plays and Players* 21 (Mar. 1974): 40–43.

Kauffman, Stanley. Rev. of *Sizwe Banzi Is Dead* and *The Island,* by Athol Fugard. *New Republic* 21 Dec. 1974: 16+.

Mackay, E. Anne. "Fugard's *The Island* and Sophocles' *Antigone* within the Parameters of South African Protest Literature." *Literature and Revolution.* Ed. David Bevan. Amsterdam: Rodopi, 1989. 145–62.

"Roadshow Back from Uganda." *Weekly Review* 30 Jan. 1981: 41.

Wertheim, Albert. "Political Acting and Political Action: Athol Fugard's *The Island.*" *World Literature Written in English* 26.2 (Autumn 1986): 245–52.

A LESSON FROM ALOES

Benson, Mary. "Fugard's *A Lesson from Aloes:* An Introduction." *Theater* 11.2 (Spring 1980): 5–6.

Collins, Michael J. "The Sabotage of Love: Athol Fugard's Recent Plays." *World Literature Today* 57.3 (Summer 1983): 369–71.

Durbach, Errol. "Surviving in Xanadu: Athol Fugard's *A Lesson from Aloes.*" *ARIEL* 20.1 (Jan. 1989): 5–21.

"The Fertility of Despair: Fugard's Bitter Aloes." *Meanjin* 40.4 (Dec. 1981): 472–79.

Wertheim, Albert. "The Lacerations of Apartheid: *A Lesson from Aloes.*" *Text and Presentation.* Ed. Karelisa Hartigan. Lanham: UP of America, 1988. 211–28.

"MASTER HAROLD" . . . AND THE BOYS

Amato, Rob. "Fugard's Confessional Analysis: *Master Harold . . . and the Boys.*" *Momentum: On Recent South African Writing.* Ed. M. J. Daymond, J. U. Jacobs, and Margaret Lenta. Pietermaritzburg: U of Natal P, 1984. 198–214.

Collins, Michael J. "The Sabotage of Love: Athol Fugard's Recent Plays." *World Literature Today* 57.3 (Summer 1983): 369–71.

Collins, William B. "A Master's Play of Tragic Import Is Brought Here." *Philadelphia Inquirer* 21 May 1982: M1.

Czarneck, Mark. Rev. of *"Master Harold" . . . and the boys,* by Athol Fugard. *Maclean's* 26 Sept. 1983: 70.

"Dance Marathon." *Time* 17 May 1982: 86.

Donahue, Francis. "Apartheid's Legacy: Athol Fugard." *Midwest Quarterly* 36.3 (1995): 323–30.

Gainor, J. Ellen. "'A World without Collisions': Ballroom Dance in Athol Fugard's 'Master Harold' . . . and the boys." *Bodies of the Text: Dance as Theory, Litera-*

ture as Dance. Ed. Ellen W. Goellner. New Brunswick: Rutgers UP, 1994. 125–38.

Gussow, Mel. "Athol Fugard Looks at a Master–Servant Friendship." *New York Times* 21 Mar. 1982: D6.

Hoegberg, David E. " '*Master Harold*' . . . *and the boys:* Succession in Fugard and Shakespeare." *Comparative Drama* 29 (Winter 1995–96): 415–35.

Kerr, Walter. "*Medea* and *Master Harold* Bring Fire to Broadway." *New York Times* 16 May 1982: D8.

Kroll, Jack. "Masters and Servants." *Newsweek* 29 Mar. 1982: 52.

Llevyld, Joseph. "*Master Harold* Stuns Johannesburg Audience." *New York Times* 24 Mar. 1983: C17.

"Masterful Fugard: Athol Fugard's '*Master Harold*' . . . *and the boys.*" *Yale Reports* 6.4 (1982): 1–2.

Olivier, G. "Notes on Fugard's '*Master Harold*' . . . *and the boys.*" *Standpunte* 35.162 (Dec. 1982): 9–14.

Richards, Frank. Rev. of "*Master Harold*". . . *and the boys,* by Athol Fugard. *New York Times* 5 May 1982: n.pag.

Roberts, Sheila. " 'No Lessons Learnt': Reading the Texts of Fugard's *A Lesson from Aloes* and '*Master Harold*' . . . *and the boys.*" *English in Africa* 9.2 (Oct. 1982): 27–33.

Simon, John. "Two Harolds and No Medea." *New York* 17 May 1982: 76.

Sutton, Brian. "Fugard's '*Master Harold*' . . . *and the boys.*" *Explicator* 54 (Winter 1996): 120–23.

Wertheim, Albert. "Ballroom Dancing, Kites, and Politics: Athol Fugard's '*Master Harold*' . . . *and the boys.*" *SPAN* 30 (Apr. 1990): 141–55.

MY CHILDREN! MY AFRICA!

Blumberg, Marcia. "Fragmentation and Psychosis: Fugard's *My Children! My Africa!*" *Madness in Drama.* Themes in Drama. 15. Ed. James Redmond. Cambridge: Cambridge UP, 1993. 241–53.

Gray, Stephen. " 'Between Me and My Country': Fugard's *My Children! My Africa!* At the Market Theatre, Johannesburg." *New Theatre Quarterly* 6.21 (Feb. 1990): 25–30.

Visser, Nicholas. "Drama and Politics in a State of Emergency: Athol Fugard's *My Children! My Africa!*" *Twentieth Century Literature* 39.4 (Winter 1993): 486–502.

PEOPLE ARE LIVING THERE

Cardullo, Bert. "Fugard's *People Are Living There.*" *Explicator* 42.4 (Summer 1984): 56–57.

————. "Patterns of Opposition in *People Are Living There.*" *Notes on Contemporary Literature* 16.1 (Jan. 1986): 39–44.

Kroll, Jack. Rev. of *People Are Living There,* by Athol Fugard. *Newsweek* 29 Mar. 1971: 121.

A PLACE WITH THE PIGS

Collerman, Jeanne. "*A Place with the Pigs:* Athol Fugard's Afrikaner Parable." *Modern Drama* 33.1 (Mar. 1990): 82–92.

Kroll, Jack. Rev. of *A Place with the Pigs,* by Athol Fugard. *Newsweek* 13 Apr. 1987: 79.

PLAYLAND

Christiansen, Richard. "Playland Shows Apartheid's Aftereffects on Black and White." *Chicago Tribune* 12 Dec. 1992, sec. 16: 2.

Holloway, Miles. "*Playland:* Fugard's Liberalism." *Unisa English Studies* 31.1 (Apr. 1993): 36–42.

Oliver, Edith. Rev. of *Playland,* by Athol Fugard. *New Yorker* 28 June 1993: 95.

Simon, John. Rev. of *Playland,* by Athol Fugard. *New York* 21 June 1993: 71.

THE ROAD TO MECCA

Blumberg, Marcia. "Women Journeying at the Margins: Athol Fugard's *The Road to Mecca.*" *Matatu* 11 (1994): 39–50.

Bowker, Veronica. "The Evolution of Critical Responses to Fugard's Work, Culminating in a Feminist Reading of *The Road to Mecca.*" *Litterator* 11.2 (Aug. 1990): 1–16.

Durbach, Errol. "Paradise Lost in the Great Karoo: Athol Fugard's *The Road to Mecca.*" *ARIEL* 18.4 (Oct. 1987): 3–20.

Heller, Janet Ruth. "The Artist as an Outcast and a Mother in *The Road to Mecca.*" *Twentieth Century Literature* 39.4 (Winter 1993): 473–78.

Kroll, Jack. Rev. of *The Road to Mecca,* by Athol Fugard. *Newsweek* 2 May 1988: 73.

Wertheim, Albert. "The Darkness of Bondage, the Freedom of Light: Athol Fugard's *The Road to Mecca.*" *Essays in Theatre* 5.1 (Nov. 1986): 15–25.

SIZWE BANSI IS DEAD

Billington, Michael. Rev. of *Sizwe Bansi Is Dead,* by Athol Fugard. *Guardian* 9 Jan. 1974: n.pag.

Blumenthal, Eileen. Rev. of *Sizwe Bansi Is Dead* and *The Island,* by Athol Fugard. *Educational Theatre Journal* 27 (1975): 416–18.

Brink, Andre. "'No Way Out': *Sizwe Bansi Is Dead* and the Dilemma of Political Drama in South Africa." *Twentieth Century Literature* 39.4 (Winter 1993): 438–54.

Ferguson, Ian. "*Sizwe Bansi Is Dead.*" *Unisa English Studies* 11.1 (Apr. 1973): 95–102.

Hammond, Jonathan. "A South African Season: *Sizwe Bansi, The Island,* and *Statements.*" *Plays and Players* 21 (Mar. 1974): 40–43.

Kauffman, Stanley. Rev. of *Sizwe Bansi Is Dead* and *The Island,* by Athol Fugard. *New Republic* 21 Dec. 1974: 16+.

Okafor, C. G. "Of Spooks and Virile Men: Patterns of Imperialism in *Sizwe Bansi Is Dead* and *The Trial of Dedan Kimathi.*" *Commonwealth Essays and Studies* 12.1 (Autumn 1989): 87–94.

Peterson, Kristen H. "The Problem of Identity in a South African Context." *ACLALS Bulletin* (1974): 10–16.

Seymour, Hilary. "*Sizwe Bansi Is Dead:* A Study of Artistic Ambivalence." *Race and Class* 21 (1980): 273–89.

Walder, Dennis. "*Sizwe Bansi.*" *The Varied Scene: Aspects of Drama Today.* Walton Hall, Milton Keynes: Open UP, 1977. 67–79.

STATEMENTS AFTER AN ARREST UNDER THE IMMORALITY ACT

Baker-White, Robert. "Authority and Jouissance in Fugard's *Statements after an Arrest under the Immorality Act.*" *Text and Performance Quarterly* 12.3 (July 1992): 228–44.

Hammond, Jonathan. "A South African Season: *Sizwe Bansi, The Island,* and *Statements.*" *Plays and Players* 21 (Mar. 1974): 40–43.

Hobson, Harold. Rev. of *Statements,* by Athol Fugard. *Sunday Times* 27 Jan. 1974: 29.

Wardle, Irving. Rev. of *Statements,* by Athol Fugard. *Times* 23 Jan. 1974: 13.

TSOTSI

Cohen, Derek. "Beneath the Underworld: Athol Fugard's *Tsotsi.*" *World Literature in English* 23.2 (Spring 1984): 273–84.

Gray, Stephen. "The Coming into Print of Athol Fugard's *Tsotsi.*" *Journal of Commonwealth Literature* 16 (Aug. 1981): 56–63.

Hough, Barrie. "Fugard's *Tsotsi:* The Missing Novel." *English in Africa* 5.2 (1978): 74–80.

Post, Robert M. "Journey toward Light: Athol Fugard's *Tsotsi.*" *College Language Association Journal* 26.4 (June 1983): 415–21.

VALLEY SONG

Bellington, Michael. "The Foundations of Dashed Dreams." *Guardian* 6 Feb. 1996: C2.

Christiansen, Richard. "As Times Are A'Changing, So Is the Playwright: Fugard in Touching *Valley Song*." *Chicago Tribune* 17 May 1996: C13.

Gener, Randy. "A Song for the New World." *American Theatre* 13 (Jan. 1996): 10.

Winer, Laurie. "*Valley Song* Takes an Uneven Look at Post-Apartheid." *Los Angeles Times* 21 May 1996: F2+.

South Africa and Apartheid

"After Apartheid." *The Christian Century* 8 Nov. 1995: 1036–37.

Anzovin, Steven. *South Africa: Apartheid and Divestiture*. The Reference Shelf. 5.1. New York: Wilson, 1987.

Barry, Ian. *Living Apart: South Africa under Apartheid*. San Francisco: Chronicle, 1996.

Biko, Steve. "The Definition of Black Consciousness." *Steve Biko—I Write What I Like: A Selection of Writings*. Ed. Aelred Stubbs. San Francisco: Harper, 1986. 48–53.

Clines, Francis X. "South Africa Tries to Prepare Those It Long Denied Ballot." *New York Times* 12 July 1994, late ed.: A1+.

Crankshaw, Owen. *Race, Class, and the Changing Division of Labor under Apartheid*. New York: Routledge, 1997.

———, and Caroline White. "Racial Desegregation and Inner City Decay in Johannesburg." *International Journal of Urban and Regional Research* 19 (Dec. 1995): 622–38.

Davies, Geoffrey, ed. *Theater and Change in South Africa*. Contemporary Theater Studies. 12. Newark: Gordon and Breach, 1996.

Davies, Robert. *Struggle for South Africa: A Reference Guide to Movements, Organizations, and Institutions*. Vol. 2. Atlantic Highlands: Humanities International, 1984.

Dayley, Suzanne. "De Klerk's Party Quits Government." *New York Times* 10 May 1996, late ed.: A1.

———. "South Africa Losing Battle to House Homeless." *New York Times* 3 May 1996, late ed.: A1.

DeGruchy, John W. "Sharpeville Revisited." *Christian Century* 26 Apr. 1995: 447.

"Dramatically Speaking, Apartheid Was Better." *Economist* 22 July 1995: 72–80.

Erasmus, Chris. "The Far Right Vows a Fight to the Death." *World Press Review* 41 (Mar. 1994): 12–13.

Fredrickson, George M. *Black Liberation: A Comparative History of Black Ideologies in the United States and South Africa*. New York: Oxford UP, 1996.

"Freedom Charter." *Black Scholar* 24 (Summer 1994): 44–47.

French, Howard W. "Everyone's Too Busy to Be Africa's Leader." *New York Times* 9 July 1995, late ed.: A16.

Fuchs, Anne. *Playing the Market: The Market Theatre, Johannesburg, 1976–1986.* Contemporary Theater Ser. 1. Newark: Gordon and Breach, 1990.

Gevisser, Mark. "South African Theater Faces a New World." *New York Times* 14 Aug. 1994, late ed., sec. 2: 5.

Gilbert, Leah. "Urban Violence and Health—South Africa 1995." *Social Science and Medicine* 43.5 (Sept. 1996): 873–86.

Grieg, Robert. "New Freedoms in South Africa May Reorient Theater." *New York Times* 27 Feb. 1994, late ed.: A12+.

Gunner, Liz, ed. *Politics and Performance: Theater, Poetry, and Song in Southern Africa.* Bloomington: Indiana UP, 1995.

Hatchen, William A. *The Press and Apartheid: Repression and Propaganda in South Africa.* Ann Arbor: Books on Demand, 1984.

Herbst, Jeffrey Ira. "Creating a New South Africa." *Foreign Policy* 94 (Spring 1994): 120–25.

Horn, Miriam. "Theater As Weapon." *U.S. News and World Report* 4 July 1988: 50–54.

Internal Commission of Jurists. *South Africa: Human Rights and the Rule of Law.* Ed. Geoffrey Bindman. London: Pinter, 1988.

Johnson, R. W. "Whites in the New South Africa." *Dissent* 43 (Summer 1996): 134–37.

Keegan, Timothy J. *Colonial South Africa and the Origins of Racial Order.* Reconsiderations in South African History Ser. Charlottesville: UP of Virginia, 1997.

Keller, Bill. "A Farmer, but Not Exactly a Boer. You See. . . ." *New York Times* 11 Aug. 1993, late ed.: A4.

———. "Next for the New South Africa: Potholes and Taxes." *New York Times* 9 July 1994, late ed.: A3.

———. "A Post-Apartheid Nightmare: Hospitals Swamped." *New York Times* 29 Aug. 1994, late ed.: A4.

———. "Rival Visions of Freedom Split South African Zulus." *New York Times* 4 Apr. 1994, late ed.: A1+.

Kirk, Joyce E. *South Africa: Race and Residence.* Boulder: Westview, 1996.

Lambley, Peter. *The Psychology of Apartheid.* Athens: U of Georgia P, 1980.

Lawrence, John C. *Race Propaganda and South Africa.* London: Victor, 1979.

Leiberman, Susan. "Jumping into Madness: South Africa's Market Theatre against Apartheid." *Theatre Crafts* 19 (Oct. 1985): 38–41+.

Leslie, Michael. "Bitter Monuments: Afrikaners and the New South Africa." *Black Scholar* 24 (Summer 1994): 33–39.

Lester, Alan. *From Colonization to Democracy: A New Historical Geography of South Africa.* New York: St. Martin's, 1996.

Lutterback, Claus. "Visions for a New Era." *World Press Review* 42 (Aug. 1995): 45.

Marx, Anthony M. *Lessons of the Struggle: South African Internal Opposition, 1960–1990.* New York: Oxford UP, 1992.

McKay, Gillian. "Drama of Dissent." *Maclean's* 18 June, 1990: 58+.

McLarin, Kimberly J. "The Voice of Apartheid Goes Multicultural." *New York Times* 25 July 1995, late ed.: A2.

Menaker, Drusilla. "A Brand New Experience in the Townships: Banking." *Business Weekly* 13 Nov. 1995: 123.

Moutout, Corinne. "Exit Apartheid." *World Press Review* 40 (Feb. 1993): 48.

Muriel, Horrell. *South Africa: Basic Facts and Figures.* Johannesburg: Institute on Race Relations, 1973.

O'Brien, Conor Cruise, and Patrick O'Brien. "Timing Is Everything." *New Republic* 1 Dec. 1986: 9–10.

Ohlson, Thomas, and Stephen John Stedman, with Robert Davies. *The New Is Not Yet Born: Conflict Resolution in Southern Africa.* Washington: Brookings, 1994.

O'Meara, Dan. *Forty Lost Years: The Apartheid State and the Politics of the National Party, 1948–1994.* Athens: Ohio UP, 1997.

Omer-Cooper, J. D. *History of Southern Africa.* London: Currey, 1987.

Pedder, Sophie. "Coming of Age: A Survey of South Africa." *Economist* 20 May 1995: 1–26.

Posel, Deborah. *The Making of Apartheid 1948–1961.* Oxford: Clarendon, 1991.

Quarshie, Hugh. "Art and Africans." *West Africa* 22 June 1981: 1410+.

Reuters. "South Africa Murders Soar." *New York Times* 18 Apr. 1996, late ed.: A10.

Ruby, Michael. "Peace Prize II for Mandela?" *U.S. News and World Report* 17 Oct. 1994: 92.

"South Africa's Muddle: Drift of the Beloved Country." *World Press Review* 42 (Jan. 1995): 8–14.

Sparks, Allister. *Mind of South Africa.* New York: Ballantine, 1991.

———. *Tomorrow Is Another Country: The Inside Story of South Africa's Road to Change.* Chicago: Chicago UP, 1996.

Steenkamp, Anton J. "The South African Constitution of 1993 and the Bill of Rights: An Evaluation in Light of International Human Rights Norms." *Human Rights Quarterly* 17 (Feb. 1995): 101–26.

Stengel, Richard. "Bazooka Joe." *New Republic* 30 Jan. 1995: 12.

Stubbs, Aelred, ed. *Steve Biko—I Write What I Like: A Selection of Writings.* San Francisco: Harper, 1986. 48–53.

Thompson, Leonard. *A History of South Africa.* 1990. New Haven: Yale UP, 1995.

———, and Monica Wilson, eds. *The Oxford History of South Africa.* 2 vols. London: Oxford, 1971.

Treiman, Donald J., Matthew McKeever, and Eva Fodor. "Racial Differences in Occupational Status and Income in South Africa, 1980–91." *Demography* 33 (Feb. 1996): 111–32.

Turnley, David, and Alan Cowell. *Why Are They Weeping?: South Africans under Apartheid*. New York: Stewart, Tabori, & Chang, 1988.

UNESCO. *Apartheid*. Paris: UNESCO, 1972.

Van den Berghe, Pierre. *South Africa: A Study in Conflicts*. Los Angeles: U of California P, 1967.

Wall, James M. "Tutu's Peace Protest Provides Ray of Hope." *Christian Century* 17 Apr. 1985: 371–72.

Weinberger, Caspar W. "Hope for South Africa—and the World." *Forbes* 15 Mar. 1993: 39.

Whitaker, Mark. "Cry, the South African Writer." *Newsweek* 4 Aug. 1986: 29.

Zimmerman, Reinhard, ed. *Southern Cross: Civil Law and Common Law in South Africa*. New York: Oxford UP, 1996.

Electronic and Media Sources

FILM AND VIDEO

Beyond Apartheid: South Africa's Quest for a Common Culture. Inquiring Mind. 21. Prod. Washington Commission for the Humanities. Narr. Gordon Jackson. Videocassette. Perspective and Reality, 1994.

Children of Apartheid. Narr. Walter Cronkite. Videocassette. California Newsreel, 1987.

Fugard, Athol. Interview. *Arts on 1*. South African Television (SATV), Johannesburg. 10 June 1992.

Generations of Resistance. Filmstrip. Southern Africa Media Center/California Newsreel, 1979.

Have You Seen Drum Lately? Exec. Prod. J. R. A. Bailey. Videocassette. Films for the Humanities and Sciences, 1995.

The Last Days of Apartheid. Dir./Prod. Greg Bowen and Rick Turner. Videocassette. Churchill Media, 1994.

Nelson Mandela. Dir. Bryan Russo. Prod. Jose Pretlow, Marlaine Walsh Sleip, and Lillian Smith. Videocassette. Films for the Humanities, 1990.

"Master Harold" . . . and the boys. Dir. Michael Lindsay-Hogg. Perf. Matthew Broderick, Zakes Mokae, and John Kami. Videocassette. Lorimar, 1984.

Ordinary People. Videocassette. First Run/Icarus, 1993.

Presentation [of Fairfield University] Bellarmine Medal of Honor to Athol Fugard. Videocassette. Fairfield University Media Center, 1985.

Sizwe Bansi Is Dead. Prod. British Broadcasting. Perf. Jose Ferrer, Ossie Davis, and Ruby Dee. 1978. Videocassette. Insight Media, 1992.

South Africa Now. Prod. Globalvision and the Africa Fund. Videocassette. WNET-NY, 1990.

Spear of the Nation: The Story of the African National Congress. Dir./Prod. Ian Stuttard and David Tereshchuk. 1986. Videocassette. Films for the Humanities, 1993.

SOUND RECORDINGS

Blood Knot. Perf. Zakes Mokae and Athol Fugard. Audiocassette. Caedmon, 1986.
Earplay 1980. Audiocassette. National Public Radio, 1980.
Fugard, Athol. *Athol Fugard: White South African Playwright.* Audiocassette. NPR, 1986.
Presentation [of Fairfield University] Bellarmine Medal of Honor to Athol Fugard. Audiocassette. Fairfield University Media Center, 1985.

CD-ROM

Apartheid and the History of the Struggle for Freedom in South Africa. Windows 3.1 version. CD-ROM. Mayibuye Books Series. Mayibuye Center: U of the Western Cape, 1994.

WWW SITES

AdmiNet. *South Africa.* 1996. Online posting. Internet. 11 Feb. 1997. Available http://www.adminet.com/world/za/.
Brians, Paul. *Study Guide for "Master Harold"... and the boys.* n.d. Online posting. Internet. 11 Feb. 1997. Available http://www.wsu.edu:8080/~brians/anglophone/fugard.html.
"Elms." *Brown Alumni Monthly.* July 1995: n.pag. Online posting. Internet. 11 Feb. 1997. Available http://www.hunger.brown.edu/Administration/Brown_Alumni_Monthly/7-95/Elms.
Fugard, Athol. *Graduation Ceremony Address, University of the Witwatersrand, 29th March 1990.* n.d: n.pag. Online posting. Internet. 5 Feb. 1997. Available http://sunsite.wits.ac.za/wits/alumni/290390.html.
Manoim, Irwin, ed. *Electronic Mail and the Guardian.* 5 Jan. 1997: n.pag. Online posting. Internet. 5 Jan. 1997. Available http://www.mg.co.za/mg/.
Mdseai, A. *About South Africa.* Dec. 1995. Online posting. Internet. 11 Feb. 1997. Available http://www.geocities.com/SiliconValley/2193/saf1.html.
Milde, Frank. *The Island Fotos.* n.d.: n. pag. Online posting. Internet. 11 Feb. 1997. Available http://www.tu-chemnitz.del~milde/Island/Island.html.
The Star. 5 Jan. 1997: n.pag. Online posting. Internet. 5 Jan. 1997. Available www.inc.coza/online/star/.

Appendix:
Documenting Sources

Documentation is the acknowledgment of information from an outside source that you use in a paper. In general, you should give credit to your sources whenever you quote, paraphrase, summarize, or in any other way incorporate borrowed information or ideas into your work. Not to do so— on purpose or by accident—is to commit **plagiarism,** to appropriate the intellectual property of others. By following accepted conventions of documentation, you not only help avoid plagiarism, but also show your readers that you write with care and precision. In addition, you enable them to distinguish your ideas from those of your sources and, if they wish, to locate and consult the sources you cite.

Not all ideas from your sources need to be documented. You can assume that certain information—facts from encyclopedias, textbooks, newspapers, magazines, and dictionaries, or even from television and radio—is common knowledge. Even if the information is new to you, it need not be documented as long as it is found in several reference sources and as long as you do not use the exact wording of your source. Information that is in dispute or that is the original contribution of a particular person, however, *must* be documented. You need not, for example, document the fact that Arthur Miller's *Death of a Salesman* was first performed in 1949 or that it won a Pulitzer Prize for drama. (You could find this information in any current encyclopedia.) You would, however, have to document a critic's interpretation of a performance or a scholar's analysis of an early draft of the play, even if you do not use your source's exact words.

Students of literature use the documentation style recommended by the Modern Language Association of America (MLA), a professional organization of more than twenty-five thousand teachers and students of English and other languages. This method of documentation, the one that you should use any time you write a literature paper, has three components: *parenthetical references in the text, a list of works cited,* and *explanatory notes.*

Parenthetical References in the Text

MLA documentation uses references inserted in parentheses within the text that refer to an alphabetical list of works cited at the end of the paper. A typical **parenthetical reference** consists of the author's last name and a page number.

> Gwendolyn Brooks uses the sonnet form to create
> poems that have a wide social and aesthetic range
> (Williams 972).

If you use more than one source by the same author, include a shortened title in the parenthetical reference. In the following entry, "Brooks's Way" is a shortened form of the complete title of the article "Gwendolyn Brooks's Way with the Sonnet."

> Brooks not only knows Shakespeare, Spenser, and
> Milton, she also knows the full range of African-
> American poetry (Williams, "Brooks's Way" 972).

If you mention the author's name or the title of the work in your paper, only a page reference is necessary.

> According to Gladys Margaret Williams in "Gwendolyn
> Brooks's Way with the Sonnet," Brooks combines a
> sensitivity to poetic forms with a depth of emotion
> appropriate for her subject matter (972-73).

Keep in mind that you use different punctuation for parenthetical references used with *paraphrases and summaries,* with *direct quotations run in with the text,* and with *quotations of more than four lines.*

Paraphrases and Summaries

Place the parenthetical reference after the last word of the sentence and before the final punctuation:

> In her works Brooks combines the pessimism of Mod-
> ernist poetry with the optimism of the Harlem Re-
> naissance (Smith 978).

Direct quotations run in with the text

Place the parenthetical reference after the quotation marks and before the final punctuation:

> According to Gary Smith, Brooks's A Street in
> Bronzeville "conveys the primacy of suffering in the
> lives of poor Black women" (980).

> According to Gary Smith, the poems in A Street in
> Bronzeville, "served notice that Brooks had learned
> her craft . . ." (978).

> Along with Thompson we must ask, "Why did it take
> so long for critics to acknowledge that Gwendolyn
> Brooks is an important voice in twentieth-century
> American poetry?" (123)

Quotations set off from the text

Omit the quotation marks and place the parenthetical reference one space after the final punctuation.

> For Gary Smith, the identity of Brooks's African-
> American women is inextricably linked with their
> sense of race and poverty:
>> For Brooks, unlike the Renaissance poets,
>> the victimization of poor Black women be-
>> comes not simply a minor chord but a pre-
>> dominant theme of A Street in Bronzeville.
>> Few, if any, of her female characters are
>> able to free themselves from a web of
>> poverty that threatens to strangle their
>> lives. (980)

[Quotations of more than four lines are indented ten spaces (or one inch) from the margin and are not enclosed within quotation marks. The first line of a single paragraph of quoted material is not indented further. If you quote two or more paragraphs, indent the first line of each paragraph three additional spaces (one-quarter inch).]

SAMPLE REFERENCES

The following formats are used for parenthetical references to various kinds of sources used in papers about literature. (Keep in mind that the parenthetical reference contains just enough information to enable readers to find the source in the list of works cited at the end of the paper.)

An entire work

> August Wilson's play <u>Fences</u> treats many themes fre-
> quently expressed in modern drama.

[When citing an entire work, state the name of the author in your paper instead of in a parenthetical reference.]

A work by two or three authors

> Myths cut across boundaries and cultural spheres and
> reappear in strikingly similar forms from country to
> country (Feldman and Richardson 124).

> The effect of a work of literature depends on the
> audience's predispositions that derive from member-
> ship in various social groups (Hovland, Janis, and
> Kelley 87).

A work by more than three authors

> Hawthorne's short stories frequently use a combi-
> nation of allegorical and symbolic methods (Guerin
> et al. 91).

[The abbreviation *et al.* is Latin for "and others."]

A work in an anthology

> In his essay "Flat and Round Characters" E. M.
> Forster distinguishes between one-dimensional char-
> acters and those that are well developed (Stevick
> 223–31).

[The parenthetical reference cites the anthology (edited by Stevick) that contains Forster's essay; full information about the anthology appears in the list of works cited.]

A work with volume and page numbers

> In 1961 one of Albee's plays, <u>The Zoo Story,</u> was
> finally performed in America (Eagleton 2:17).

An indirect source

> Wagner observed that myth and history stood before
> him "with opposing claims" (qtd. in Winkler 10).

[The abbreviation *qtd. in* (quoted in) indicates that the quoted material was not taken from the original source.]

A play or poem with numbered lines

> "Give thy thoughts no tongue," says Polonius,
> "Nor any unproportioned thought his act"
> (<u>Ham.</u> 1.3.59-60).

[The parentheses contain the act, scene, and line numbers, separated by periods. When included in parenthetical references, titles of the books of the Bible and well-known literary works are often abbreviated—*Gen.* for *Genesis* and *Ado* for *Much Ado about Nothing,* for example.]

> "I muse my life-long hate, and without flinch / I
> bear it nobly as I live my part," says Claude McKay
> in his bitterly ironic poem "The White City" (3-4).

[Notice that a slash [/] is used to separate lines of poetry run in with the text. The parenthetical reference cites the lines quoted.]

The List of Works Cited

Parenthetical references refer to a **list of works cited** that includes all the sources you refer to in your paper. (If your list includes all the works consulted, whether you cite them or not, use the title *Works Consulted.*) Begin the works cited list on a new page, continuing the page numbers of the paper. For example, if the text of the paper ends on page six, the works cited section will begin on page seven.

Center the title *Works Cited* one inch from the top of the page. Arrange entries alphabetically, according to the last name of each author (or the first word of the title if the author is unknown). Articles—*a, an* and *the*—at the beginning of a title are not considered first words. Thus, *A Handbook of Critical Approaches to Literature* would be alphabetized under *H*. In order to conserve space, publishers' names are abbreviated—for example, *Harcourt* for Harcourt Brace College Publishers. Double-space the entire works cited list between and within entries. Begin typing each entry at the left margin, and indent subsequent lines five spaces or one-half inch. The entry itself generally has three divisions—author, title, and publishing information—separated by periods.*

A book by a single author

> Kingston, Maxine Hong. <u>The Woman Warrior: Memoirs of a Girlhood among Ghosts.</u> New York: Knopf, 1976.

A book by two or three authors

> Feldman, Burton, and Robert D. Richardson. <u>The Rise of Modern Mythology.</u> Bloomington: Indiana UP, 1972.

[Notice that only the *first* author's name is in reverse order.]

A book by more than three authors

> Guerin, Wilfred, et al., eds. <u>A Handbook of Critical Approaches to Literature.</u> 3rd. ed. New York: Harper, 1992.

[Instead of using *et al.*, you may list all the authors' names in the order in which they appear on the title page.]

Two or more works by the same author

> Novoa, Juan-Bruce. <u>Chicano Authors: Inquiry by Interview,</u> Austin, U of Texas P, 1980.

---

* The fourth edition of the *MLA Handbook for Writers of Research Papers* (1995) shows a single space after all end punctuation.

---. "Themes in Rudolfo Anaya's Work." Address
given at New Mexico State University, Las
Cruces. 11 Apr. 1987.

[List two or more works by the same author in alphabetical order by title.
Include the author's full name in the first entry; use three unspaced hyphens
followed by a period to take the place of the author's name in second and
subsequent entries.]

An edited book

Oosthuizen, Ann, ed. <u>Sometimes When it Rains: Writings by South African Women.</u> New York: Pandora,
1987.

[Note that the abbreviation *ed.* stands for *editor.*]

A book with a volume number

Eagleton, T. Allston. <u>A History of the New York
Stage.</u> Vol. 2. Englewood Cliffs: Prentice.
1987.

[All three volumes have the same title.]

Durant, Will, and Ariel Durant. <u>The Age of Napoleon:
A History of European Civilization from 1789 to
1815.</u> New York: Simon, 1975.

[Each volume has a different title. *The Age of Napoleon* is Volume II of *The
Story of Civilization.*]

A short story, poem, or play in a collection of the author's work

Gordimer, Nadine. "Once upon a Time." <u>"Jump" and
Other Stories.</u> New York: Farrar, 1991. 23–30.

A short story in an anthology

Salinas, Marta. "The Scholarship Jacket." <u>Nosotros:
Latina Literature Today.</u> Ed. Maria del Carmen

> Boza, Beverly Silva, and Carmen Valle. Bingham-
> ton: Bilingual, 1986. 68-70.

[The inclusive page numbers follow the year of publication. Note that here the abbreviation *Ed.* stands for *Edited by*.]

A poem in an anthology

> Simmerman, Jim. "Child's Grave, Hale County, Ala-
> bama." The Pushcart Prize, X: Best of the Small
> Presses. Ed. Bill Henderson. New York: Penguin,
> 1986. 198-99.

A play in an anthology

> Hughes, Langston. Mother and Child. Black Drama An-
> thology. Ed. Woodie King and Ron Miller. New
> York: NAL, 1986.399-406.

An article in an anthology

> Forster, E. M. "Flat and Round Characters." The The-
> ory of the Novel. Ed. Philip Stevick. New York:
> Free, 1980. 223-31.

More than one selection from the same anthology

If you are using more than one selection from an anthology, cite the anthology in one entry. In addition, list each individual selection separately, including the author and title of the selection, the anthology editor's last name, and the inclusive page numbers.

> Kirszner, Laurie G., and Stephen R. Mandell, eds.
> Literature: Reading, Reacting, Writing. 3rd ed.
> Fort Worth: Harcourt, 1997.
> Rich, Adrienne. "Diving into the Wreck." Kirszner
> and Mandell. 874-76.

A translation

> Carpentier, Alejo. Reasons of State. Trans. Francis
> Partridge. New York: Norton, 1976.

An article in a journal with continuous pagination in each issue

```
LeGuin, Ursula K. "American Science Fiction and the
     Other." Science Fiction Studies 2 (1975):
     208-10.
```

An article with separate pagination in each issue

```
Grossman, Robert. "The Grotesque in Faulkner's
     'A Rose for Emily.'" Mosaic 20.3 (1987): 40-55.
```

[20.3 signifies volume 20, issue 3.]

An article in a magazine

```
Milosz, Czeslaw. "A Lecture." The New Yorker 22 June
     1992: 32.
"Solzhenitsyn: An Artist Becomes an Exile." Time
     25 Feb. 1974: 34+.
```

[34+ indicates that the article appears on pages that are not consecutive; in this case the article begins on page 34 and then continues on page 37. An article with no listed author is entered by title on the works cited list.]

An article in a daily newspaper

```
Oates, Joyce Carol. "When Characters from the Page
     Are Made Flesh on the Screen." New York Times
     23 Mar. 1986, late ed.: C1+.
```

[C1+ indicates that the article begins on page 1 of Section C and continues on a subsequent page.]

An article in a reference book

```
"Dance Theatre of Harlem." The New Encyclopaedia
     Britannica: Micropaedia. 15th ed. 1987.
```

[You do not need to include publication information for well-known reference books.]

```
Grimstead, David. "Fuller, Margaret Sarah." Encyclo-
     pedia of American Biography. Ed. John A. Gar-
     raty. New York: Harper, 1974.
```

[You must include publication information when citing reference books that are not well known.]

A CD-ROM: Entry with a print version

> Zurbach, Kate. "The Linguistic Roots of Three
>   Terms." <u>Linguistic Quarterly</u> 37 (1994): 12-47.
>   <u>Infotrac: Magazine Index Plus.</u> CD-ROM. Informa-
>   tion Access. Jan. 1996.

[When you cite information with a print version from a CD-ROM, include the publication information, the underlined title of the database (*Infotrac: Magazine Index Plus*), the publication medium (CD-ROM), the name of the company that produced the CD-ROM (Information Access), and the electronic publication date.]

A CD-ROM: Entry with no print version

> "Surrealism." <u>Encarta 1996.</u> CD-ROM. Redmond: Micro-
>   soft, 1996.

[If you are citing a part of a work, include the title in quotation marks.]

> <u>A Music Lover's Multimedia Guide to Beethoven's 5th.</u>
>   CD-ROM. Spring Valley: Interactive, 1993.

[If you are citing an entire work, include the underlined title.]

An online source: Entry with a print version

> Dekoven, Marianne. "Utopias Limited: Post-sixties
>   and Postmodern American Fiction." <u>Modern Fic-
>   tion Studies</u> 41.1 (Spring 1995): 121-34. On-
>   line. Internet. 17 Mar. 1996.
> Available http://muse.jhu.edu/journals/MFS/v041/41.1
>   dekoven.html.

[When you cite information with a print version from an online source, include the publication information for the printed source, the number of pages (*n. pag.* if no pages are given), the publication medium (Online), the name of the computer network (Internet), and the date of access. If you wish, you may also include the electronic address, preceded by the word *Available.* Information from a commercial computer service—America Online, Prodigy, and CompuServ, for example—will not have an electronic address.]

O'Hara, Sandra. "Reexamining the Canon." <u>Time</u> 13 May
    1994: 27. Online. America Online. 22 Aug. 1994.

An online source: Entry with no print version

"Romanticism." <u>Academic American Encyclopedia.</u> On-
    line. Prodigy. 6 Nov. 1995.

[This entry shows that the material was accessed on November 6, 1996.]

An online source: Public Posting

Peters, Olaf. "Studying English through German."
    29 Feb. 1996. Online Posting. Foreign Language
    Forum, Multi Language Section. CompuServe.
    15 Mar. 1996.
Gilford, Mary. "Dog Heroes in Children's Litera-
    ture." 4 Oct. 1996. Newsgroup alt.animals.dogs.
    America Online. 23 Mar. 1996.

[**WARNING:** Using information from online forums and newsgroups is
risky. Contributors are not necessarily experts, and frequently they are
incorrect and misinformed. Unless you can be certain that the information you are receiving from these sources is reliable, do not use it in your
papers.]

An online source: Electronic Text

Twain, Mark. <u>The Adventures of Huckleberry Finn.</u>
    From <u>The Writing of Mark Twain.</u> Vol. 13.
    New York: Harper, 1970. Online. Wiretap.
    spies. Internet. 13 Jan. 1996. Available
    http.//www.sci.dixie.edu/DixieCollege/Ebooks/
    huckfin.html.

[This electronic text was originally published by Harper. The name of the
repository for the electronic edition is Wiretap.spies.]

An online source: E-Mail

Adkins, Camille. E-Mail to the author. 8 June 1995.

An interview

> Brooks, Gwendolyn. "Interviews." <u>Triquarterly</u> 60
>   (1984): 405-10.

A lecture or address

> Novoa, Juan-Bruce. "Themes in Rudolfo Anaya's Work."
>   New Mexico State University, Las Crues, 11 Apr.
>   1987.

A film or videocassette

> "<u>A Worn Path.</u>" By Eudora Welty. Dir. John Reid and
>   Claudia Velasco. Perf. Cora Lee Day and Con-
>   chita Ferrell. Videocassette. Harcourt, 1994.

[In addition to the title, the director, and the year, include other pertinent information such as the principal performers.]

Explanatory Notes

Explanatory notes, indicated by a superscript (a raised number) in the text, may be used to cite several sources at once or to provide commentary or explanations that do not fit smoothly into your paper. The full text of these notes appears on the first numbered page following the last page of the paper. (If your paper has no explanatory notes, the works cited page follows the last page of the paper.) Like works cited entries, explanatory notes are double-spaced within and between entries. However, the first line of each explanatory note is indented five spaces (or one-half inch), with subsequent lines flush with the left-hand margin.

TO CITE SEVERAL SOURCES

In the paper

> Surprising as it may seem, there have been many
> attempts to define literature.[1]

In the note

[1] For an overview of critical opinion, see Arnold 72; Eagleton 1-2; Howe 43-44; and Abrams 232-34.

TO PROVIDE EXPLANATIONS

In the paper

In recent years gothic novels have achieved great popularity.[3]

In the note

[3] Gothic novels, works written in imitation of medieval romances, originally relied on supernatural occurrences. They flourished in the late eighteenth and early nineteenth centuries.

Credits

822
Fugard

Fugard, Athol.

"Master Harold"-- and
the boys.

$11.95

DATE			

BAKER & TAYLOR